# Praise for *Born on the Fourth of July* by Ron Kovic

"Ron Kovic's memoir is a classic of antiwar literature."
—Howard Zinn, author of
*A People's History of the United States*

"As relevant as ever, this book is an education. Ron is a true American, and his great heart and hard-won wisdom shine through these pages." —Oliver Stone, filmmaker

"A great courageous fellow, a man of deep moral convictions and an uncompromising disposition."
—Secretary of State John Kerry

"Ron Kovic is one of the premier voices of a generation. The large irony of his birthday provides the background for a journey which begins with the unquestioning service in Vietnam, his terrible wounding with all the anger and bitterness that follows, and ends with his passionate discovery of a large and all too human heart. I'll say this flat out: If you want to understand the everlasting reverberations of our war in Vietnam and how it impacts our current events, you must read this book." —Larry Heinemann, author of *Paco's Story*, winner of the National Book Award

". . . the most personal and honest testament published thus far by any young man who fought in the Vietnam War . . . And what is so remarkable about Kovic's writing is that whereas one is perfectly prepared to forgive him occasional lapses into bitterness, self-pity or excesses of rage, he retains the most extraordinary self-control throughout. He very patiently, meticulously, unself-consciously defines the sort of background he came from . . . Only by understanding Kovic's working class credentials can one begin to comprehend the depth of betrayal he has every right to feel."
—*New York Times (Editors' Choice)*

# HURRICANE STREET

# HURRICANE STREET

# RON KOVIC

Published by Akashic Books
©2016 Ron Kovic

Hardcover ISBN: 978-1-61775-449-4
Paperback ISBN: 978-1-61775-450-0
Library of Congress Control Number: 2015954057

First printing

Akashic Books
Twitter: @AkashicBooks
Facebook: AkashicBooks
E-mail: info@akashicbooks.com
Website: www.akashicbooks.com

*for* TerriAnn Ferren

# Contents

*To care for him who shall have borne the battle and for his widow and his orphan . . .*
—President Abraham Lincoln,
Second Inaugural Address, March 4, 1865

This is the story of a few brave men who, though severely wounded in war, returned home to fight a different battle.

# Introduction

Over forty years have now passed since that day in 1974 when we first entered the office of Senator Alan M. Cranston of California and began a sit-in which would quickly escalate into a hunger strike and touch the nation. *Hurricane Street* is a work of both memory and fiction. It is my own recollection of the strike and all that followed that spring and summer. Some names and details have been changed out of respect for people's privacy, and to fill gaps in my memory. (One such memory gap is a meeting that took place early in the strike with Senator Cranston on February 13, 1974. Unfortunately, nothing substantive came of that meeting, which is probably why it didn't lodge itself in my memory, and why I have not included it in this book.) For the sake of presenting a coherent story line, I have also taken the liberty of creating two characters: Tony D., who is essentially a composite of several sight-impaired Vietnam veterans I knew while I was a patient at the Bronx and Long Beach VA hospitals; and Joe Hayward, who represents a number of seriously wounded veterans I also knew during that period. In addition, I have combined the two AVM takeovers of the Washington Monument in the spring and summer of 1974 into one single action.

Each night during the strike after the lights were turned out, I would make entries in my diary using a small penlight. Some of the entries were very brief while others were quite long. Back then I sensed the need, even in the most minimal way, to record the history of the strike. I figured somebody had to try to tell this story while they still could. Most of us, including myself, didn't expect to live very long back then, with all the nightmares and anxiety attacks screaming in our heads. No doubt everyone involved will have their own way of remembering those days and giving their opinions on what may or may not have happened, but this is how I remember it.

**R**evolution was in the air. The cities were burning as National Guardsmen patrolled the streets with fixed bayonets, taking sniper fire from rooftops. It was an extraordinary time, an agonizing time, a time of great conflict, a time of great sorrow, and a time that would forever change the way we saw our country and the world. America seemed to be tearing itself apart; never before had the nation been so polarized; not since the Civil War had we as a people been so divided. Everything was being questioned, nothing was sacred, even the existence of God was now suspect. The very earth beneath my feet seemed to be shifting, and there no longer seemed to be any guarantees, or anything that could be trusted or believed in anymore.

*As the last American troops were being withdrawn from Vietnam in the spring of 1974, a small group of disabled veterans staged a two-week hunger strike at the West Los Angeles office of then–US Senator Alan Cranston.*
—Elaine Woo, *Los Angeles Times*, August 13, 1999

This is the story of that strike.

# PART I

## THE HOSPITAL

The first thing that hits you in this place is the smell. It is a terrible odor of urine and feces, of human bodies all crammed into these depressing little cubicles. There are no private rooms, just these filthy green curtains separating the paralyzed men in their hospital beds. It is like a huge warehouse of human refuse, a storage center for the living dead. There is talk of building a new facility but the funds are just not there. They must all go to the war effort, a war we cannot win, a war where young men continue to die and are maimed for nothing, for a lost cause.

As paralyzed veterans, we all walk a very thin line between being on the outside and stuck in this place. It is not an easy wound to live with. There are the bedsores and the catheters, the urinary tract infections and high fevers, the lack of sexual function, spasms, and terrible insomnia that torments you in the night. Each morning you wake up wondering how you're going to make it through another day. There is an entire body that does not move or feel from your midchest down and you are constantly lifting yourself up from your cushion in your wheelchair to keep your skin from breaking down. You're scared and try your best to hide all that you've lost, all that you're going through.

Do the American people, the president, the politicians, senators, and congressmen who sent us to this war have any idea what it really means to lose an arm or a leg, to be paralyzed, or to begin to cope with the psychological wounds of that war? Do they have any concept of the long-term effects of these injuries, how the struggles of the wounded are only now just beginning? How many will die young and never live out their lives because of all the stress and the myriad of problems that come with sending young men into combat?

You struggle to look normal—to fit into this world again after all that has happened to you. It all seems so overwhelming at first, but somehow you find a way to continue on. There are the anxiety attacks and the horrifying nightmares, the depression and thoughts of giving up. You do your best. You've got to keep living. You've got to keep getting up every morning no matter how crazy it all seems. You're amazed that you're still alive, that after all the frustrations and confinement, in and out of bed, fevers, IVs, wetting your pants, soiling the sheets, you are still here, still in this world.

You try to sit proudly in your wheelchair every day, try not to lose your balance. It is incredible how normal a person can look if he only tries. You do your best to get back into life again but you know deep down inside that nothing will ever be the same, that you have lost more than most people could ever imagine, sacrificed more for your country, short of dying, than most of your fellow citizens could ever comprehend.

# The SCI Ward

D
r. M., the chief surgeon at the hospital's Spinal Cord Injury (SCI) Center, walks past me. He is very tired but still he recognizes me and says hello. He has been in the operating room all day. His first patient, a paraplegic from D ward, had to have a flap put on his rear end for a bedsore that wouldn't heal. There are a lot of them in here with that problem and sometimes the flap doesn't take and they have to do it all over again. It can be very frustrating. Dr. M.'s second patient was not as lucky and had to have his gangrenous left foot removed. The nurses did all they could to save the foot but in the end they just weren't able to. There are a lot of paralyzed guys around here with amputated legs. You can get a really bad burn and not even know it. I remember hearing a story once about a guy who came home drunk one night with his girlfriend and she filled the bathtub and placed him in it, not realizing the water was scalding hot. He got burned really badly and died the following week. There are a lot of stories like that and you try to never forget them. These are important lessons, and as

horrible as it may seem, remembering them is crucial to our survival.

For nearly three months last year I was a patient here at the Long Beach VA hospital, healing a terrible bedsore on my rear end after a fall in the bathtub at my apartment. The accident happened not long after I had broken up with a woman named Carol who I first met at an antiwar demonstration in Los Angeles in the spring of 1972. Carol was the first woman I loved and the very first woman to break my heart. After we broke up I felt as if my whole world had fallen apart.

I was depressed and hardly getting any sleep at night. I remember putting a bandage over the bruise but it just kept getting worse. After a while the bruise became a sore and the sore an open wound, until finally I had to turn myself in to the hospital.

The last place I wanted to be was back in the Long Beach VA hospital. I hated the place. The conditions were atrocious, as bad if not worse than the Bronx VA in New York where I had been after I first came home from the war. The wards were overcrowded and terribly understaffed. The aides would sit in their little room at the end of the hall drinking coffee and cackling away as men on the wards cried out for help that never came. All the windows were tightly shut. The air was rancid, and I would push my call button again and again but no one would come to help.

The anger and frustration would build up inside me and I remember several times screaming into my pillow as I lay on my gurney until I was exhausted. I felt so helpless, so lost. During the entire time, in that depressing place, Carol never called or came down to visit me once. I felt abandoned, betrayed, and soon stopped shaving and began to let my hair grow long. I remember looking in the mirror one morning thinking how much I resembled Jesus Christ hanging from the cross. I thought back again to the Bronx VA when I had been stuck in that chest cast for nearly six months after breaking my femur, and how as I had lain on a gurney on my stomach I would paint pictures of the crucifixion with myself as Christ, and how they'd sent the psychiatrist down from the psych ward because they were concerned and I immediately stopped painting, afraid they would have me committed just like my Uncle Paul who had been beaten to death in a mental hospital years before.

The weeks and months in the Long Beach VA hospital passed, and I slowly began to adjust to my surroundings. Each morning the aides would lift me out of bed and place me on a gurney, stuffing a pillow under my chest to keep my testicles from squishing and my hips from getting red. They would do the same thing with my legs, placing another pillow under my kneecaps, making sure my bed bag was hooked up, then handing me my two wooden canes. Lying on the gurney on my stomach I'd push around the wards, then down to the cafeteria where I'd get something to eat. I would then go outside on the grass where I'd throw bits of crackers to the sparrows. This became a daily routine for me.

In the weeks that followed I began to make new friends. Many, like myself, had been paralyzed in Vietnam, guys like Marty Stetson and Willy Jefferson, Woody and Nick, Danny Prince and Jake Jacobs, or Jafu as he liked to be called, who used to be a bodybuilder before he joined the marines. Jafu, I learned from Marty, was wounded in Operation Starlite on August 23, 1965, while participating in America's first major offensive of the Vietnam War. He was shot in the chest, paralyzing him from his waist down. From what Marty told me, Jafu's squad got caught in a horseshoe ambush, and though gravely wounded, Jafu continued to return fire with his M60 machine gun until reinforcements arrived. For this he was awarded a Silver Star and Purple Heart.

Nick Enders shares a completely different story, though, telling me Jafu was actually paralyzed while on R&R in Hawaii. Some guy caught him sleeping with his wife and in a jealous rage threw him out of the sixth-floor window of his hotel room, paralyzing Jafu for life. I don't know which story is true but I try not to ask too many questions. In a place like this, those things don't seem to matter.

Of the new friends I've made at the hospital, Jafu is probably the quietest of the bunch, saying very little and letting his grunting and groaning down in the physical therapy room speak for itself. A runner-up in the Mr. Universe contest before the war, Jafu could bench press 250 pounds and now boasts he will soon be lifting three hundred pounds as a paraplegic. He has an incredible physique. From his waist up, his bulging muscles remind me of a championship boxer or wrestler. In high school he ran the hundred-yard dash in 9.7 seconds and set a school record.

Jafu refuses to accept the fact that his paralysis is permanent. He is convinced that given enough time, determination, and effort he will be able to overcome his injury. He talks about it all the time and has even hired a Chinese herbalist on the outside who says he can help. The man prescribes herbal medicines, everything from devil's claw to capsaicin, arnica to coca leaves. Jafu takes all sorts of vitamins and supplements, convinced his spine can be fused together through a proper diet and physical regimen.

He speaks of experiments with rats in Canada that he has read about in *Reader's Digest* where, miraculously, the animals' severed spines have been regenerated. Like everyone else in this place, Jafu has his hopes and dreams. As soon as he gets out of the hospital he plans to move to Hawaii and open a weightlifting gym on Waikiki Beach where he will continue his journey toward walking again. I have often seen him sitting in his wheelchair alone in the hallway, staring off into the distance, seeming terribly lost and deep in thought. I want to go up to him but I hesitate. There are just some things a man needs to figure out for himself.

While most of us here have accepted our fate and know our wounding in the war is permanent, Jafu refuses to believe that he will never walk again. For the most part we support him, encouraging him, even if we all know it's just his way of coping. A person has a right to keep on hoping; no one wants to take away Jafu's dreams. In a place like this, there must be hope, and even Jafu's stubbornness and denial give us all something to believe in.

I understand why Jafu feels the way he does. When I was at the Bronx VA in New York back in 1968, I was determined to walk again no matter what. I was young, twenty-one years old, and though initially devastated by my paralysis, I was convinced like Jafu that with enough hard work and determination I could walk again. I told the doctors I wanted braces, and at first they resisted, explaining to me that my idea of walking again was unrealistic if not impossible and that the level of my injury, T4–T6, was too high and dragging my paralyzed body around with braces and crutches would surely prove to be too strenuous.

Refusing to accept their verdict, I continued to insist that they allow me to have the braces—explaining that as a 100 percent service-connected combat vet who had just sacrificed three-quarters of his body in Vietnam, I deserved the opportunity to try to walk again. For the next few weeks I continued to ask for the braces, even threatening to call the media and hold a press conference on the Spinal Cord Injury ward unless they followed through with my request. Eventually the doctors relented and about a month later I received the braces.

I can still remember the first time I put the braces on in the ADL (activity of daily living) room with the help of my two physical therapists, Dick Carter and Jimmy Ford. I was so excited and couldn't wait to get up on my feet. Carefully positioning myself behind the parallel bars, I grabbed ahold of both bars and in one quick motion lifted myself out of my wheelchair, and, with the help of my braces, stood in an upright position for the first time since my injury.

I felt a bit weak and shaky at first but it was wonderful to be standing again, even if I couldn't feel anything from my midchest down and had to imagine where my lower body and feet were. With Jimmy and Dick guiding me, I began to drag myself step by step as far as I could along the parallel bars until I was exhausted.

"It's beautiful up here!" I remember shouting to no one in particular, thrilled at the renewal of my old vantage point.

Every day after that I arrived at the ADL room early to put on my braces. I would then begin my daily routine, dragging my paralyzed body back and forth between the parallel bars, determined to do my very best.

By the second week I had already left the confines and safety of the parallel bars and begun to venture around the ADL room, proudly dragging my lifeless body past the others in their wheelchairs and no longer afraid to set out on my own. Each day, as I grew more and more confident and my stamina increased, so did my determination to go farther.

By the third week I was now dragging my body down the hall and onto the paraplegic ward, visiting the other patients in their rooms and confounding many of the doctors and nurses who had earlier dismissed my belief that I would walk again.

I said hello to everyone, including a few of the doctors and nurses who had warned me that for a high-level injury like my own—no use of my stomach muscles, and a spine that had been severed by a bullet—the odds against me walking again, much less even getting up on my feet, were astronomical. Some of them looked at me like I was crazy while still others chose to simply ignore me, turning their heads as I dragged myself past them. Of course, back then as a fiercely determined, twenty-one-year-old former Marine Corps sergeant just back from a war and a former high school athlete, I believed I could accomplish anything I set out to do. As far as I was concerned, like Jafu, nothing was impossible.

I remember telling Jimmy Ford several weeks later that the only way I was going to leave the hospital was on my feet. "I'm going to walk out of this place, Jimmy, if it's the last thing I do!"

By late November of 1968, having been in the hospital a little over eleven months and my rehab now complete, I was finally ready to be released. I'll always remember that last day at the hospital: Dick and Jimmy helping me put on my braces one last time, awkwardly dragging my body with my crutches out of the ADL room, Dick spotting me all the way across the hall and into the elevator where we rode down to the ground floor. "You can do it, Ronnie! You can do it. Careful, Ronnie. Careful now!"

I had only a little farther to go before I reached the SCI parking lot where my brand-new hand-controlled Oldsmobile was parked. I struggled, dragging myself across the gravel lot, growing more and more determined—doing my best not to fall . . . trying not to lose my balance.

"A little bit farther. A little bit farther! Keep going, Ronnie! Almost there, Ronnie!" shouted Dick. "Only a little more to go."

When we finally reached the car I leaned forward, still balancing myself on the crutches, and unlocked the door, and after opening it slowly I spun around, swinging myself into the seat. "I did it, Dick!" I shouted. "I told you I was going to walk out of this place." I had triumphed. I had done it.

After returning home to Massapequa, Long Island, I continued my rehabilitation, putting on braces every day, and just as I had dragged myself around the hospital, I now began to drag my body around the yard each day, seeing how far I could go, determined to continue my struggle to walk again.

It was great to be home and as I progressed each day I would sometimes notice the neighbors staring over from their front lawns or out their windows at the neighborhood boy who had returned from the war with the terrible wound, desperately trying to walk again. I did my best to put them at ease, waving to them and smiling as I awkwardly struggled to keep my balance and not fall. I didn't want them to feel sorry for me. As difficult and frustrating as it was for me each day, I chose to see it as a great physical challenge rather than a burden. Even back then I was trying hard to see things in a more positive light. I was still the great athlete striving to win the championship, to be my very best and make the Olympics and win a gold medal.

And although I fell several times in my yard that summer, each time I was able to get myself back up and continue on.

One afternoon, just as the summer was ending, I remember my mother peering through the dining room window with the saddest look on her face I had ever seen, as I once again struggled to drag myself around the yard. She had watched me try to walk in my braces many times before, encouraging me and telling me how proud she was, but on this afternoon she was no longer able to hide her sorrow.

Years later, my mother would confide that seeing me for the first time attempting to walk with my braces in my backyard, occasionally losing my balance, falling and picking myself up, reminded her of Jesus Christ and the Stations of the Cross.

I would try to smile, lifting one of my crutches above my head and shaking it in a show of triumph to let her know everything was okay, but my mother just kept staring at me, seeming as if she was about to cry.

"What's wrong, Mom?" I asked her when I got back into the house later that day, but all she could do was continue to look at me with those sad eyes, telling me how it hurt her to see me struggling each day, my body all twisted and atrophied, dragging myself exhausted around the yard.

"It really hurts me to see you out there. It's too much, Ronnie. It's too much. Maybe the doctors were right. Maybe you should just accept the fact that you've got to be in a wheelchair. It's not good for you. It's too much of a strain on your heart. I watch you, Ronnie, and it hurts me. I love you, Ronnie. I just don't want to see you suffer anymore."

I had hoped that my mother would continue to be encouraging and supportive of my attempt to walk again. Didn't she and the others understand what I was trying to do? I tried not to let the neighbors' uneasy stares and my mother's sadness and doubts bother me, but by the end of that summer I was putting on the braces and dragging myself around the yard less and less, feeling depressed and spending more time getting drunk at Arthur's Bar.

One night in late August I came home very drunk and pushed myself back into my house, up the wooden ramp my father had built when I was at the hospital. I pushed my wheelchair down the hallway to my room, trying not to wake my mother and father or any of my brothers and sisters. When I got there, I sat in my wheelchair staring at myself in the mirror for a long time, thinking back to the promise I had made to myself and the others in the Bronx VA hospital that I would walk again.

I had not taken my braces out of the closet or tried to walk in several months, but on that night I was determined to get up again. Sometime after midnight, I took the braces out of the closet, transferred into my bed, and put the braces on, locking them in place. I then transferred back into my wheelchair, grabbed my crutches, and lifted myself slowly out of my chair into an upright position. After taking a deep drunken breath, I began to stubbornly drag myself around the room. I had only gone a few steps when I found myself facing the mirror once again. I remember staring at my twisted and atrophied body and with one last superhuman effort, refusing to be defeated, I spun around angrily, dragging myself across the floor of my room. After several steps I lost my balance and went crashing to the floor. I thought for a moment of getting up again, of making one last vain attempt to walk, but I was too tired and drunk and instead I began to cry, tears streaming down my face, hoping my mother and father wouldn't hear me. A few minutes later I pulled myself back into my wheelchair where I slowly unstrapped my braces and threw them into the closet.

I know the truth is that someday they will find a way to fuse the spine together, but not in my lifetime or the lifetime of the others around me. Our job here is to keep on living, to keep getting up and making it through each day any way we can.

# It's Fucking Scary in Here

My new group of friends at the Long Beach VA and I start getting together almost every day in back of D ward, sharing our thoughts and feelings about the war and the treatment we're receiving at the hospital. Many speak of outright patient abuse, while others, like Marty and Willy, say they were punished for complaining about their treatment. I have been told that several patients have already been sent to the psychiatric ward because they complained. Marty says this is common practice by the staff to keep everyone in line.

"There are a lot of things that happen here that no one ever talks about," Marty tells me, taking a swig from his whiskey bottle hidden inside a paper bag. "Accidents that no one will ever report."

Marty Stetson is by far the most sarcastic and cynical of us all. Whenever Jafu brings up the subject of walking again, Marty goes crazy. "You're never going to fucking walk again!" he scolds. "You gotta just accept your fucking injury, man. This fucking thing's never gonna change."

With his long hair and wispy Ho Chi Minh beard, his emaciated body lying naked on his filthy sheet, he looks more like a survivor of Auschwitz than a Vietnam veteran. Marty is haunted by the war. His sad, mournful eyes say it all. A former Army Airborne Ranger who was shot and paralyzed in Pleiku in 1968, he seems to have given up on life. He speaks listlessly and without emotion, a scratchy whine that is both pathetic and stirs great compassion at the same time. It is a desperate sort of crying out for help.

He once showed me a photograph of himself in his Ranger uniform with a parachute on his chest from when he was at jump school in Fort Bragg, North Carolina. It was just before he went to Vietnam. In the photo Marty looks really confident.

Marty's been drinking a lot lately, Jim Beam whiskey. It's his favorite. He used to ask me, when I was still in my chair, to go across the street to the liquor store and pick him up a bottle. I'd return it to him in a paper bag but I had to be careful; if they caught me bringing alcohol into the hospital I could get in a lot of trouble. I know it's not good for Marty but who am I to judge? He has been trapped in his bed for nearly six months now with a terrible bedsore on his right hip. Ever since I met him he's been in bed trying to heal that sore. It occurred when one of the aides dropped him in the shower room. Marty said the aide was drunk and had come close to dropping him several times before.

When you have a bedsore like this, you have to be

disciplined and stay in bed. You're stuck there twenty-four hours a day, seven days a week. You can't get up. You become completely dependent on the people around you. It's not easy. You start to go crazy. You feel trapped. Some of the guys like Marty can't take it anymore and they start drinking or using drugs. Marty's been seeing one of the dietitians from the second floor and she's started supplying him with drugs—marijuana, cocaine, uppers, downers, LSD . . . you name it.

Some guys become impatient and get up into their chairs. This only prolongs the problem and the sore gets even worse. Eventually the bone begins sticking out, and infection, high fever, and septic shock can set in; many patients have already died from this. It is an overwhelming and constant struggle to stay on top of this thing.

Everyone has his own way of dealing with it. Sometimes you hear screaming and cursing. Others just lie silently on their gurneys—"doing their time," as they call it, any way they can. Some talk to the chaplain, others the ward psychologist, but most just try their best to endure.

Marty's been in for surgery twice already but he refuses to stay in bed. He keeps getting up and making excuses. The bedsore is getting worse and an infection has already set in. The doctors and nurses repeatedly tell him that he's got to stay in bed, but Marty doesn't seem to care. He's tired of doing time and seems incapable of the discipline and self-control it takes to heal a bedsore. He doesn't want to talk about it and he doesn't want to think about it. Instead, he gets lost in his music and alcohol and drugs.

He loves Jimi Hendrix and listens to him a lot. He's also a fan of the Animals' song "We Gotta Get Out of This Place." He plays it again and again and says whenever it was played on Armed Forces Radio in Vietnam all the guys in his squad would start singing it.

"I love this fucking song!" shouts Marty, tears streaming down his face as he turns up the volume of his headset full blast, closes his eyes tightly, and dreams of the day he'll finally escape. *"We gotta get out of this place if it's the last thing we ever do,"* he mumbles. *"We gotta get out of this place 'cause girl, there's a better life for me and you. Now my girl you're so young and pretty and one thing I know is true, yeah. You'll be dead before your time is due,"* he sings, slurring his words, his eyes still tightly shut, his head swaying back and forth, lost in another world, place, and time, far from the hospital and the paraplegic ward.

And then there's Nick, another paralyzed vet I meet at the hospital. While Marty seems to keep much of his rage inside, getting high and losing himself in his music, Nick is much more expressive and outgoing. An army combat medic and Bronze Star recipient, Nick survived an entire tour of duty only to be shot and paralyzed during a liquor store holdup in Compton, California. From what I heard, he had been back from Vietnam a little less than a year when it all happened. He couldn't sleep at night, couldn't hold a job, had a hard time concentrating, and eventually ended up broke and homeless, living in his station wagon in a parking lot near Venice Beach. He went down to the VA for a couple of sessions with one of the psychiatrists but it didn't seem to help. Nick told me the guy fell asleep on him and started snoring just when Nick was telling him about a friend who died in his arms after being shot in an ambush. When Nick accused the guy of dozing off, the shrink denied it, claiming instead that he was deep in thought. Nick never went back to him again.

A few weeks later, Nick had a breakdown and ended up in a locked psychiatric ward at the Long Beach VA suffering from hallucinations, flashbacks, and severe insomnia. I've heard he was put in a straitjacket and confined to a darkened room where he was given psychotropic drugs and zonked out on Thorazine.

After several weeks he was finally released and returned to living at the beach in his station wagon. One thing led to another, and hungry, desperate, broke, out of gas, Nick hitchhiked to his old neighborhood in Compton, attempted to rob a liquor store with an unloaded gun he had picked up at a pawn shop, and was shot in the back by one of the clerks, paralyzing him for life. The judge, citing mitigating circumstances—his Bronze Star, Purple Heart, and heroic record as a combat medic in Vietnam—eventually dropped the charges. Nick did his rehabilitation at the Long Beach VA Spinal Cord Injury Center.

The first time I met Nick was in the back of C

ward. They've got a pool table set up there. It's sort of a recreation room for the guys donated by the local VFW. Everyone was crowded around the table in their wheelchairs and Nick was shooting pool. He loves being the center of attention. I remember he made this incredible shot using just one hand, holding the pool cue with no bridge. He was trying to sink the eight ball and nobody thought he could do it. "Ladies and gentlemen, I am about to make one of the greatest pool shots in the history of the world, and I will do it with one hand and both eyes closed. Would anyone like to bet against me?" Nick is a great pool player and quite frankly a bit of a hustler too. Betting's not allowed in the hospital but Nick supposedly cleared over two hundred dollars that day.

Before the war, Nick was a struggling stand-up comic and would often perform on the Ocean Front Walk in Venice Beach with a dummy that he picked up one Sunday at a flea market. He named the dummy Edgar after the famous ventriloquist Edgar Bergen who Nick says was his inspiration.

Nick hides his depression well. His moods swings are extreme and, when not hyperexcitedly talking about his latest scheme, he can often be found alone in his hospital room, staring out the window, looking like a frightened child. When I see him like this, I want to reach out to him, try to comfort him, but in the end I wheel away. He reminds me too much of my own horrors and torments, all the terrible guilt and shame I continue to suppress and keep well hidden.

Nick's kindness and desire to be there for others is constantly on display. Forever the combat medic, he roams the SCI ward in his wheelchair most of the day looking to comfort his fellow Vietnam veterans. He is always ready to lend a helping hand, glad to assist his brothers in need whenever possible, whether it's listening to their many problems or racing down to the PX in his wheelchair to pick up a much-needed item for someone stuck in bed. The busier Nick is, the happier he seems to be. For now, his demons and thoughts of suicide, always lurking just below the surface, can wait. In this swirl of frantic activity his tortured soul can find relief, at least for a while.

For all of Nick's generosity and concern for his brothers, as he affectionately calls them, he has little time to care for himself. Deeply troubled and plagued by hallucinations and nightmares, he bounces from one frightening day to the next.

We continue to meet in the back of D ward and, as I get to know my new friends better, I also start sharing more of my own story. I tell them about the Bronx VA and the May 1970 *Life* magazine article, "Our Forgotten Wounded." Several of them say they saw it. I tell them about the overcrowded conditions in the Bronx, the rats on the ward, urine bags overflowing onto the floor, the paralyzed men left lying in their own excrement for hours at a time, crying out for help that never comes. I tell them about Mark D., the quadriplegic Vietnam vet depicted in the magazine, sitting naked in his shower chair next to a garbage can with nothing but a dirty towel covering his private parts. I explain how it was Mark who had written a letter to *Life* telling them of the disgraceful conditions on the Bronx VA paraplegic ward and pleading with them to do something about it. Finally they did respond, with a disturbing photo exposé that shocked the public and infuriated the bureaucrats at the VA. There were numerous denials and letters to the editor attacking Mark and the magazine for "exploiting" our wounded veterans. After receiving threats against his life, Mark eventually left the VA and moved back to Chicago where he lived with his parents for a while before eventually taking his own life in 1971.

We meet in the back of D ward over the next few weeks, and it is during this period that I decide to begin my own one-man investigation of the Long Beach VA SCI ward. I buy a tape recorder at the hospital PX, with batteries and extra cassettes, and begin to formulate a plan. I will hide the tape player under the pillow on my gurney. I have to be careful. If they find out what I'm doing, there could be severe repercussions. They might try to punish me like some of the others who complained. No one must know what I'm up to.

At first I visit only patients I can trust—some are the guys I've been meeting with in back of D ward. Marty, Nick, and Willy Jefferson are the first to be interviewed. I then begin to branch out to other wards, expanding my investigation to more patients, including some of the aides and one doctor who I know is on our side.

Many complain of overcrowded conditions while others say that something must be done before another patient dies. "It's fucking scary in here," a patient from D ward tells me one afternoon as he leans forward to whisper into my microphone.

Some talk about the failure of medical devices: Hoyer lifts that suddenly stop working during the transfer of a patient, and IV pumps and blood pressure machines that are constantly breaking down. One veteran, a quad from C ward, begins to cry while telling me he and several others have been threatened numerous times by one of the aides for refusing his extortion demands. The aide knows that as 100 percent service-connected combat veterans, we receive a substantial tax-free check each month from the government, and he makes it clear to the guys that if they refuse to pay and don't give him a little "gratitude" each week, they will not get the care they deserve. This goes on here all the time but no one ever talks about it. Don't get me wrong, there are some decent aides and nurses who really do care, but they are few and far between.

I continue taping as many patients as are willing to talk to me. One tells me that he was slapped by a nurse when he complained, and another that he was dropped onto the floor when two drunken aides tried to drag him from his bed onto a gurney. Some speak of what they will do when they finally get out of the hospital. I distinctly recall one young paralyzed ex–marine lieutenant named Miller describing in great detail how he planned to get on top of a building and start shooting everyone he could with his M16 rifle.

Many are tormented by nightmares and anxiety attacks and some have simply given up—surrendering to their despair and paralysis. The look of permanent defeat is etched across their faces. Young boys of nineteen and twenty, guys like Marty and Danny and Willy Jefferson, old before their time. They are weary men in every way, seeming to have lost all hope. Their lives are over, their youth has been crushed, defiled, and destroyed. Unlike myself, they do not rage. They do not protest or dream of revolt. They simply surrender to their defeat, to their paralyzed bodies.

I listen to one horror story after another and promise myself that someday people are going to know what is happening in this place. If it is the last thing I do, I will somehow find a way to expose it.

By the end of the second week, I have filled up nearly half a dozen cassette tapes. Doing the interviews and acting as an investigative reporter on my gurney has kept me busy and I have begun to feel less alone.

# The Patients'/Workers' Rights Committee

By mid-April the situation on the Spinal Cord Injury ward has become intolerable and it is during this period that I decide to start organizing a group called the Patients'/Workers' Rights Committee. We begin holding meetings every Thursday night in back of the wards. Most of our discussions have to do with the poor treatment we are receiving at the hospital and what we, as a group, can do to change it.

At first we have only a few patients, but soon our numbers begin to grow until there are over a hundred patients coming to every Thursday-night gathering. Many of those who show up are from the SCI ward, but quite a few come from other parts of the hospital. There are the World War II vets, the guys with tuberculosis wearing those yellow masks over their faces, a few Korean War vets, and several aides and nurses who have their own reasons to complain and protest. Even one of the SCI doctors shows up one night, telling us he sympathizes with us and supports what we're trying to do, but he has to be careful.

The larger we grow as a group each week, the more anxious and uncomfortable the powers-that-be at the hospital seem to become, not to mention quite a few of the more irate WWII veterans. Some despise me, calling me names as I wheel past them in the hallway: *hippie, radical, fucking Communist.* But I say nothing. The country, and even the hospital, feels terribly divided between those who still support the war and those who oppose it. Arguments often break out and emotions are raw. Many have seen me on TV or read about my previous activities as an antiwar protester in the newspapers.

Joe Hayward, who will become one of my closest allies, only to later betray me, shows up at one of our meetings, telling me that he was recently hired by the VA as a "chaplain's assistant," giving him access to many of the hospital wards. He will be helping the chaplain to write a weekly report pertaining to patients' needs, attitudes, and behaviors. He promises to share his information with us and soon he is taking an active roll in our organization.

Late that spring, we decide to hold a press conference and invite everyone from the media to attend. I even invite the actress Jane Fonda, having heard that she would be speaking next door at Long Beach State University later that same day. I am thrilled when I'm told by her representative that she can attend, and I begin making plans to let everyone in the hospital know she's coming. Jane and I had already shared the stage at several antiwar demonstrations and I know that her presence at our press conference will create quite a stir, not to mention all the additional media attention it will bring.

With an old mimeograph machine loaned to us by one of the volunteers, we set up our own printing press on one of the empty hospital beds in the back of the ward. We churn out nearly five hundred copies of a flier inviting everyone in the hospital to a press conference with Jane Fonda and the Patients'/Workers' Rights Committee, to be held the following week on the grass behind the SCI ward, where we will present our complaints gathered over the last several months.

On the pay phone down the hall, we call every local newspaper and network, alerting them to our press conference, which we say will expose the scandalous conditions at the Long Beach VA and VA hospitals all over the country.

We are surprised at the response we receive. The press seems to be interested. Some reporters want to come down right away but we tell them to hold off and wait for the press conference when we can fill them all in at once. Everyone on the committee seems excited. I plan to play some of the cassette tapes of the interviews I have done with dissenting patients to any reporters who are willing to listen. Other patients and a few aides have also volunteered to be interviewed. Nick, Woody, Bobby Mays, and I begin handing out leaflets to everyone we meet in the hospital. By the end of the week everyone at the Long Beach VA seems to be talking about Jane Fonda's impending visit and the Patients'/Workers' Rights Committee's press conference in back of the SCI ward. A small group of disgruntled World War II and Korean War veterans, incensed that Fonda is coming, make it clear that they plan to stage a counterprotest.

When the day of the press conference finally arrives, we are stunned at the number of media that turn out. They seem fascinated by it all: Actress Jane Fonda attending a press conference with severely disabled Vietnam veterans. Men who have sacrificed nearly their entire bodies, being abused and neglected at a VA hospital. What a story!

The place is packed. Everyone in the hospital seems to have shown up that day, including the small group of World War II and Korean War veterans in wheelchairs determined to disrupt the press conference. At around eleven fifteen a.m., with the press in full attendance and members of the Patients'/Workers' Rights Committee by my side, I announce that Jane Fonda is running a little late. "Miss Fonda should be here in a few minutes, and as soon as she arrives we'll begin the press conference," I say, sounding very confident.

When she finally does arrive, it's a mob scene with reporters and news camera crews rushing toward her. The World War II and Korea vets, along with their wives, immediately start shouting at Fonda: "Communist! Traitor!" Then, suddenly, almost as if on cue, they begin singing "God Bless America." For a moment it seems as if the whole thing is about to disintegrate into chaos.

Somehow, though, I am able to speak, thanking Jane Fonda for coming, and then inviting some of our Patients'/Workers' Rights Committee members to share their stories. Fonda is visibly moved and several times I notice tears running down her cheek. When it's finally her turn to speak, everyone is listening, with the exception of the counterdemonstrators, who continue to attempt to drown out our event by singing patriotic songs. Fonda starts by telling everyone how grateful she is to have been invited to attend our press conference.

"I can't begin to tell you how much respect I have for all of you and how deeply moved I am today after listening to your stories," she says, her voice beginning to crack as more tears stream down her face. "This is very wrong!" She sighs deeply and shakes her head. "This shouldn't be happening in America, not to our veterans . . . You have sacrificed so much . . . I had no idea our veterans were being treated this way." She goes on to say that she will do everything she can to get the word out concerning the crisis regarding paralyzed veterans at the VA.

When she finishes we lead her and the press onto the SCI ward where we introduce her to several bedridden patients, who because of their medical conditions could not attend the press conference but nonetheless had agreed to testify. With news cameras and reporters surrounding their bedsides and with tears in their eyes, they bravely share the harrowing ordeals they have suffered at the hands of the VA; Fonda listens intently, seeming almost in a state of shock.

Not long after Jane Fonda has left and the press conference has ended, we are all over the news. Patients everywhere in the hospital, including paraplegics and quadriplegics on the SCI ward, watch the six o'clock news from their beds as the media report, in their lead stories, that there is trouble down at the Long Beach VA.

The next morning the powers-that-be at the hospital are visibly upset. Several representatives of the hospital administration come down to our ward and start asking questions in a not-too-friendly manner. "Who started this thing?" I remember one guy in a suit and tie asking, sounding very frustrated. "What's going on down here?"

# When Will Your Funeral Be?

A few evenings later, after being transferred back into my bed on C ward, one of the aides tells me I have a phone call. Back then there was only one phone on the ward, an old clunky contraption on wheels with a long extension cord that they would have to push down to a patient's bedside when he got a call. It made a distinctive squeaky sound.

My first thought is that my ex-girlfriend Carol has finally decided to call me. I get all excited, my heart pounding in my chest, as the aide hands me the phone.

"Hello!" I say, though there is nothing but silence on the other end. "Hello?" I repeat, but still no one says a thing.

Finally, a man in a deep, gruff voice comes on the line and asks me if I am Ron Kovic.

"Yes," I say, "this is Ron Kovic."

"Well, we're calling today to find out when your funeral is. We'd really like to know when it's going to be so we can all attend."

I immediately wonder if it's someone from the LAPD Red Squad or one of the undercover cops who threw me out of my wheelchair during a protest in front of the Reelect Nixon campaign headquarters in 1972. Determined not to let him frighten me, I respond in a calm voice, "Thanks so much for calling me today, I'll definitely let you know when my funeral is!" Suddenly there's a loud click on the other end of the phone. My heart is still pounding in my chest when one of the aides finally comes by to take the phone away.

I realize at this moment how cruel these people can be, how even a marine combat veteran paralyzed from his midchest down, strapped to a gurney trying to heal a bedsore, is not exempt from their dirty tricks. Regardless, I am proud that I maintained my composure and that he was the one to hang up the phone. Not me.

I know now that I'm a target and that they can come in at any time, walk up to my bed when I'm sleeping, and kill me. How easy it would be for them to enter an open ward at any hour of the day or night and shoot me. I imagine them paying off a nurse or an aide who despises me for my political views to give me the wrong medication. Or perhaps they will get to one of the troubled vets from the psych ward and send him in to harm me.

I can hardly sleep and decide not to tell the others about the call—afraid that it might frighten them and keep them from continuing on with the struggle. I do my best to put on a brave face, but the thoughts of what could happen at times threaten to overwhelm me.

I eventually tell Bobby Mays about the phone call and he begins sleeping by my bedside every night, determined to keep others from harming me. I tell him it isn't necessary but he insists.

This is the third time my life has been threatened for protesting and speaking out. The first was at a high school on Long Island in the spring of 1971 when my very first speech against the war was interrupted by a bomb threat. The second time was after my arrest in front of the Reelect Nixon headquarters in '72 when the arresting officer threatened to throw me off the roof of the LA County jail.

When I first came to the hospital I thought, well, at least I'll get some rest from all the protests and madness going on outside this place—the demonstrations, police informants hounding our every move, our phones being tapped, etc.—but after that call, I realize this is not to be the case at all.

The following morning I push my gurney to a quiet garden in back of the ward. I feel helpless and afraid. After everything I went through in the war and the hospital, I have begun to wonder whether there is a God or not. Yet, out of sheer desperation, I start to pray. I ask God for His help and guidance, telling Him that I feel weak and frightened and don't know if I can go on. I remember pushing my face into my pillow on my gurney so no one would see me crying. I ask God to forgive the person who threatened my life and to give me the strength to continue organizing despite the threats. With tears streaming down my face I reach out, telling God how frightened I am. "I'm so scared, God. I'm sick with fear. I feel so vulnerable, so overwhelmed by all of this. Please help me, God. Please protect me."

I wipe the tears from my eyes as a feeling of peace like I have never felt before sweeps over me and I leave the garden no longer afraid, knowing now that what I am doing is the right thing. I can't explain it, but something deep within tells me that what I am doing is right, that I am in the right place at the right time and God wants me to continue my work and He will protect me . . . that I mustn't be afraid . . . I will continue to organize the Patients'/Workers' Rights Committee and hold our meetings every Thursday night, and if anyone wants to harass me and threaten my life, they can, but from now on I will not be afraid.

Whether there is a God or not, the talk today in the garden seems to have at least temporarily calmed my fears and given me a sense of strength and well being that up until this point I have lacked.

# The Threats and Intimidation Continue

Several weeks later that newfound faith and strength is tested when during one of our Thursday-night gatherings, Marty Stetson tells me there's a rumor going around the hospital that someone is planning to poison me.

"They're going to put poison in your water pitcher when you're away from your bed," Marty whispers.

I take this threat seriously though try my best not to let Marty know how frightened I feel, brushing it off and telling him to "consider the threat a compliment." And that it is clearly an indication of how effective we are becoming as an organization.

The following week someone rips the windshield wipers off my car in the SCI parking lot and a day later they flatten all my tires. I am careful not to drink from my water pitcher by my bedside anymore, choosing instead to purchase cans of Coke from the hallway vending machine. *This is crazy*, I remember thinking. *Here I am in a hospital trying to heal, to get better, and people want to kill me!*

* * *

By Memorial Day weekend 1973, my bedsore has finally healed and I am able to get into my chair again.
I feel very weak and out of shape but still thrilled to be
sitting up in my chair. I was trapped on the gurney for
nearly ninety-three days, but finally I am free and it's a
wonderful feeling.

As time passes, I grow more and more confident,
and by early June I'm finally ready to leave the hospital.

At my last meeting with the Patients'/Workers'
Rights Committee before I leave, I wish the others
well, telling them how proud I am of them and all they
have accomplished. I promise to stay in touch and let
them know that if for any reason they need me, they
can call at any time.

My plan is to head back to my hometown of Massapequa, Long Island, for some much-needed rest. The
following night Joe Hayward and another member of
the committee drive me to the airport to make sure I
get on the plane safely.

# Massapequa

urned out and exhausted, I spend most of the summer at my parents' house in Massapequa, resting up in my room and taking notes in a black-and-white composition notebook for what I hope will be my first book.

In July I receive a collect call from Nick telling me that the Patients'/Workers' Rights Committee has fallen apart, and that many of those involved are being punished. "Woody and Jafu are on the psychiatric ward. Willy and Danny are confined to their beds, being punished for complaining, and the rest of the guys are afraid to say anything! You gotta come back and help us. They really came down hard after you left and things are worse now than ever. You gotta come back, brother!" shouts Nick over the phone, sounding desperate.

I patiently listen to him, promising to return right away, but I know I won't be going back anytime soon. I am still exhausted, and besides, why would I want to return to all that madness at the VA, all the threats and intimidation?

It is summer on Long Island and I am home in Massapequa and there seems to be no better place in the world to be at this moment. I spend the remainder of July and August in my room continuing to rest and taking notes for the book that I hope to write as soon as I get back to the West Coast.

# Hurricane Street

By the end of the summer, having rested up sufficiently, I head back to California, where with the help of my friend and real estate agent Sally Baker, I rent a small house in Marina Del Rey along the ocean at 24 1/2 Hurricane Street. It is there that I hope to finally settle down and begin writing my book.

I still remember the night I put that first sheet of paper in my typewriter, thinking of all the things I wanted to say. I feel a powerful urge that's hard to describe, only that I just know I have to write this book.

I love the night and work for hours as if no time has passed at all. I am exhausted and my back aches, but none of that seems to matter. Convinced that I am destined to die young, I struggle to leave something of meaning behind, to rise above the darkness and despair.

For the next several nights I continue to write as the words flow, seeming as if they will never stop. I feel wonderful inside, tired but completely consumed by my writing. I drink a couple cups of coffee and then with a new surge of energy work for another hour or so as the bright lights of the morning begin to fill the room. I neatly stack all the pages next to the typewriter after holding them proudly in my hands, then transfer out of my wheelchair and onto my water bed.

Everything is progressing nicely when, a few nights later, for some reason I stop writing. I don't know what to do. For the next several hours I sit behind my desk waiting for the words to come—but there is nothing. I feel frustrated. I can't concentrate. *Why am I even writing this book?* I ask myself. *What am I doing here on Hurricane Street?* The truth is, I can't stop thinking about the war and the guys at the Long Beach VA hospital—Marty, Danny, Jafu, Willy, and Nick. I can't abandon them. Wasn't *I* the one who promised I would be there if they needed me? Wasn't *I* the one who said I would never let them down? I have to do something.

For a moment there was hope with the Patients'/ Workers' Rights Committee, a belief that we could make a difference and that our lives could be improved. But they had infiltrated our group, set veterans against one another, did all they could to stop us. Who do these people think they are? How dare they try to stop us from expressing ourselves. What kind of country is this? What kind of democracy is this, where men who sacrificed almost their entire bodies are kept from exercising those very rights and freedoms they supposedly fought for? I am angry. There has to be another way.

My thoughts drift, and sometime around one a.m.

I type the letters *ARM*. I sit staring at the letters, just three letters, *ARM*.

*American Revolutionary Movement,* I think to myself. *Yes, that's what I'll call it!*

ARM will be the answer. We will be the spark that will set off a raging prairie fire, sweeping away everything in its path. It will be a powerful organization, the vanguard of a great movement. Veterans from all across the country will join us. Millions will take to the streets, citizens from every walk of life, all of them will come, all of them will march with us, their fists raised high in the air, chanting and crying out for justice, for an end to this madness!

I continue to work on my idea throughout the next few days, but I soon begin to feel a queasiness in my stomach as I sit behind my rolltop desk. There is something about the name ARM that troubles me, something that makes me feel vulnerable.

Once again the nightmares return and I find myself trapped in a violent storm at sea. There is a terrible howling of the wind and a helpless feeling so profound that it leaves me shaking like a frightened child upon awakening.

At first I merely brush it off, but the next night is even worse. This time in my nightmare, a squad of heavily armed cops comes crashing through the door of my house with their guns drawn, cursing and screaming, calling me a traitor and threatening to kill me. "Get up, you fucking son of a bitch! Get up, you motherfucking Commie traitor!" yells one of the cops who looks exactly like Mr. Warden, my fifth-grade history teacher who warned us that "the Chinese Communists will someday have a billion people," and that "Americans everywhere should be afraid!" The cops then drag me out of my bed and through a long and darkened hallway into an elevator, and take me down to the ground floor, where they pull me across a lawn covered in broken glass, laughing and cursing at me, slamming me against a brick wall where they say they plan to execute me immediately. I keep screaming to them that I am paralyzed and can't stand up for the execution, and they are kind enough to provide a rickety old chair once used by the condemned Irish revolutionary James Connolly at his execution in Dublin, not long after the 1916 Easter Rising. I still remember them pointing their guns at me and firing as I jerked awake, my heart pounding in my chest.

Sensing right away what the dream means, I feel angry and frightened all at the same time. There has to be a way I can still accomplish my vision of a powerful revolutionary organization without the government cracking down on us before we even get started. How will we do it? What will be our approach? I have to be careful. I am already afraid that the government and police are tapping my phone and watching my every move. Perhaps a different, less provocative name for the group might be better.

I sit in front of my typewriter staring at the blank sheet of paper for a long time until finally I have it. It won't be called the American Revolutionary Movement; instead I will call it the American Veterans Movement. This makes sense. I remember typing the letters AVM on the paper and then feeling a great sense of relief. Finally I have the name I've been looking for, a less provocative one, but still powerful. I work feverishly that night, as if there's no time to lose. I type the words *American Veterans Movement* again and again, then the slogan, *We will fight and we will win!*

Just as quickly, I decide to design buttons and membership cards for the new organization. I draw a circle, and inside the circle I make a square with two lines through it. Above the top line I write the word *red,* in the middle the word *white,* and below the bottom line the word *blue.*

Across what is to become the red, white, and blue American flag, I write AVM in bold letters. Above the flag I write the words, *WE WILL FIGHT,* and below, *WE WILL WIN!* Outside the circle I then add, *AMERICAN VETERANS MOVEMENT.*

On the back I draw a crude map of the United States and across it I boldly print the letters AVM, giving the impression that it is a big national organization. *No one even knows we exist!* I think, laughing to myself. It's nothing more than a dream in my head as I sit alone on Hurricane Street that night.

The following morning I get up early and can't stop thinking about the AVM. After transferring out of the water bed and into my wheelchair, I head straight to my desk where I look at the drawings I did, feeling even more excited about the new organization. My mind fills with all sorts of ideas. I grab a blank sheet of paper and continue designing a membership card for the group. Across the top I type in the words, *AMERICAN VET-ERANS MOVEMENT OFFICIAL MEMBERSHIP CARD.* Below that, the obligatory name, first and last, address, phone number, and finally, at the very bottom, rank and specialty while in the service. I write down some basic rules and regulations for the new organiza-tion: veterans from every war will be welcome, no dues will be collected, and everyone will be treated equally and with the utmost respect.

That afternoon, after looking through the yellow pages, I find the AAA Flag & Banner store in Culver City. I call and ask the guy on the other end of the line if they make custom flags, banners, and buttons. "As many you want!" he exclaims.

The following morning I get in my hand-controlled car and head over to the store, all my drawings and de-signs for the AVM next to me on the front seat. I arrive around noon, transfer into my chair, wheel myself in, and am immediately met by a smiling bald-headed guy who seems to have just awakened from a nap.

"What can I do for you today?" he asks in a tired voice as he rubs the sleep from his eyes, straightening up a bit and taking a deep breath.

"I don't know if you remember, but I'm the guy who called you yesterday about the flags and banners and buttons I need to have made up." I hand him my pa-pers with all the drawings and designs, explaining to him exactly what needs to be done.

"No problem," he says.

I leave the store and head back to Hurricane Street.

About a week later I return to Culver City, hardly able to contain my excitement. I can't wait to see the finished product. The guy unfurls a thirty-foot white canvas banner, and in large, bright red letters scrawled across it are the words, *AMERICAN VETERANS MOVEMENT*, just as I had envisioned that night on Hurricane Street.

"Wow! It's beautiful!"

He then lifts a large cardboard box onto the counter filled with a number of small flags and hundreds of shiny red, white, and blue AVM buttons. The sign just above the register reads, *BELIEVE IN YOUR DREAMS*, and I think back to something I heard on the radio about how great entrepreneurs can envision their creations long before they become reality. That's exactly how I feel now.

"They're beautiful," I say to the guy. "They look just the way I hoped they would!"

All of a sudden it seems to be coming together. I thank the guy, paying him with what's left of my monthly disability check, money I should be using for rent. I drive back home with the AVM buttons, banner, flags, and membership cards in the trunk of my Oldsmobile, feeling happier than I have in a long time. My book can wait. Now I have to organize the others and turn my dream into reality.

The next morning I drive south down the 405 freeway to the Long Beach VA, where twenty minutes later I pull into the Spinal Cord Injury parking lot, transfer into my wheelchair, and head into the hospital. I really don't know where to start first, and I feel an almost overwhelming desire to tell *everyone* about the new organization. But who can I trust? Who should I approach first? These are big plans and it feels like a lot is at stake. I finally decide to go to the cafeteria, get some lunch, and take a little time to think about what to do next.

As I enter the cafeteria I spot my friend Bobby Mays sitting alone at one of the tables, staring blankly out the window.

"Hey, brother, how ya doin'?" I shout as I wheel my chair next to his.

Bobby and I first met the year before, just as I was leaving D ward one afternoon and he was walking out too. As we passed each other I remember he suddenly stopped, looked straight at me, and started shouting, "Ron Kovic? Are you Ron Kovic? I can't believe it's you!" Months before, his wife Sharon had given him a copy of the July 19, 1973 *Rolling Stone* article about me, "Ask a Marine," by the draft resister David Harris, with a large centerfold photo of me sitting in my wheelchair, taken by the photographer Annie Lebowitz. He told me he had read the article countless times and had been carrying around that issue of *Rolling Stone* in his backpack for months. "I knew it was you!" he shouted, hugging me with that tremendous enthusiasm of his, almost lifting me out of my wheelchair. How could I not love Bobby from the start? He made me feel great. He was one of the sweetest, most generous men I had ever met and even gave me the shirt off his back on several occasions when I was down and out and running low on clothes.

He had curly red hair, sparkling, intense, almost crazy blue eyes, and the handsome good looks of a movie star. "I always knew I was going to meet you someday!" he yelled. Like long-lost brothers we bonded that afternoon, and I knew we would always be friends.

Without missing a beat, Bobby talked nonstop for nearly an hour, telling me how he had become addicted to heroin while serving with the air force in Saigon, and was later arrested, tried, and sentenced to nine months of hard labor at Vietnam's infamous Long Binh Jail stockade, describing the terrible abuse he had suffered in solitary confinement.

He eventually became involved in a riot at LBJ in August of 1968. Bobby was initially accused of being one of the ringleaders of the rebellion, though the charges were eventually dropped. After finally being released from the LBJ stockade in April 1969, he was forced to serve the rest of his tour of duty before being allowed to return home.

In October of 1969 he headed back to Indiana a broken man, distrusting all authority and hooked on heroin. After wandering around for several months, depressed, homeless, and jobless, he joined the local chapter of the Vietnam Veterans against the War (VVAW), where he met the beautiful nineteen-year-old Sharon McAlester, who got him off drugs and eventually agreed to marry him.

They hitchhiked out to the West Coast in early '73 with, from what Sharon later told me, nothing more than twenty-nine dollars and the packs on their backs. Bobby was now clean and sober and got a job as a nurse's aide for one of the paralyzed veterans at the Long Beach VA and began taking caregiver classes at the hospital, determined to leave the drugs behind and straighten out his life.

He and I soon became the best of friends, with Bobby on several occasions inviting me down to his place in Long Beach for one of Sharon's delicious home-cooked meals. He would later join me in organizing the Patients'/Workers' Rights Committee and attended every meeting we had.

Bobby really missed me when I was away, telling me he got depressed after the Patients'/Workers' Rights Committee fell apart and that he's anxious to know what we plan to do next. He'd heard rumors I was back in town and wants to know about everything I've been doing. "What's up, brother? What's happening? Anything new?" he asks.

His eyes light up as I begin telling him all about the AVM. Then I share my idea of setting up a meeting with Senator Alan Cranston to discuss the conditions on the SCI ward. Later in the afternoon I show him the buttons and banners in the trunk of my car, explaining how we will get all the guys we know in the hospital to join us, and will take over the senator's office and begin a sit-in, not leaving until our demands are met.

"Will he actually meet with us?" Bobby asks.

"I don't know. That's what we're going to find out. Come on, Bobby, follow me!" I say as I wheel over to a pay phone, in that crazy and spontaneous way of mine back then, and put in a couple of quarters. "I'm calling the senator's office over at the Federal Building in Westwood right now!"

Bobby stands next to me with a curious look on his face.

"Hello, is this Senator Cranston's office? Who am I speaking with, please? . . . Hi, this is Ron Kovic and I'm a paralyzed Vietnam veteran calling from the Long Beach veterans hospital. I'm calling today because we've got some serious problems down here on the Spinal Cord Injury ward and we'd like to set up a meeting with Senator Cranston as soon as possible."

The guy, who by the sound of his voice I can tell is very young, thanks me for my service, telling me that the senator will be out of town for the next few weeks. However, the senator's aide offers to meet with us the following week on Tuesday, February 12, at two o'clock, promising that he'll take notes and share all our concerns with the senator. "Will that work for you?" he asks in a chirpy voice.

"Absolutely!" I shout back into the phone, giving Bobby the thumbs-up to let him know things are going as planned. I thank the guy, hang up the phone, take a deep breath, and explain my plan to Bobby.

"Listen, brother, this is the situation. I've set up a

meeting in Senator Cranston's office for next Tuesday at two o'clock. The senator's not going to be there, but none of that matters. What we're going to tell everyone is that we've got a meeting with Senator Cranston in his office on Tuesday. I know it's not the truth but it's the only way this thing is going to happen. All we're going to tell them is that Senator Cranston has agreed to meet with us and after the meeting we're going to take everybody out to lunch in Westwood. You can't tell them we're going to take over the office, and you can't tell them about the sit-in. If you tell the others that, they're going to completely freak out—believe me, Bobby, it's hard enough to get them out of their beds every morning, much less get them to the Federal Building in Westwood for a meeting with Senator Cranston who won't even be there."

Bobby nods his head, promising me he won't say a word. We shake hands in the way we did back then, clasping our hands tightly and staring into each other's eyes intensely to let each other know we really mean it, that this is a pact between brothers.

Bobby seems impressed while at the same time a bit concerned. "What's going to stop them from arresting us? What's to keep them from calling security?" Bobby already has several warrants for his arrest due to unpaid parking tickets. "I don't want to get busted, man. I got a wife and a kid on the way. I can't afford to go to jail, man."

I explain that Senator Cranston is up for reelection, has an important position as chairman of the Senate

Committee on Veterans' Affairs in Washington, and will more than likely be sympathetic.

"The odds are in our favor, Bobby. Can you imagine what it would look like if the cops are seen dragging a bunch of paralyzed Vietnam veterans in wheelchairs out of Senator Cranston's office and arresting them?"

Bobby smiles, seeming a bit more confident.

"Look, there's nothing to worry about, brother," I say, placing my hand on his shoulder. "Everything's going to be fine."

We shake hands again and hug each other tightly, promising to meet at the hospital the next day.

# We Organize

Bobby and I meet at the hospital the following morning, entering the Spinal Cord Injury ward from a side entrance we're both familiar with. Little has changed on the wards since I left the place nearly a year ago. Bobby and I head over to C ward to visit some of our friends. Several of them were members of the Patients'/Workers' Rights Committee and have agreed to meet with us.

Nick, Danny, Woody, and the paralyzed marine weightlifter Jafu all seem happy to see us. They fondly remember our weekly meetings, or "little rebellions" as Woody likes to call them, every Thursday night in the back of D ward last spring and how we came together and began to make a difference. All of that seems to have faded now.

Jafu is depressed. He says that ever since the Patients'/Workers' Rights Committee fell apart, things have gotten really bad. "Some of the aides and nurses started threatening the guys with lobotomies and shock treatment, handing out pills like candy, drugging those who complained, until they were too numb to speak out."

They returned to the wards broken men, docile and compliant. These same brave men who had attended the meetings of the Patients'/Workers' Rights Committee, these men who had raised their voices in protest and righteous indignation, are nowhere to be found. They have been shut up. They have been silenced by a fear that now seems to permeate the entire place. They had just begun to discover themselves, just begun to feel strong. These once proud men have been broken and discarded. The spark of hope that had slowly begun to emerge out of that deep dark chasm of depression and defeat now seems to have been extinguished. The feeling of dignity and pride and self-worth that had begun to grow, the faith that just maybe something good could come of all this, that perhaps even a victory of sorts, like the one that had been denied them in the war, could become a reality—all of that is gone now, all of that has been destroyed by those who fear them. They are beaten men and a look of permanent defeat now covers their faces.

Woody says that after I left they tried their best to keep the organization going. "We kept having our meetings every week and for a while it looked like we could really make a difference. But the security guards kept harassing us, taking our pictures from their van with their long-range lenses. We tried not to let it bother us—"

"They sent in informants too," interrupts Jafu. "Patients from other wards who pretended they supported us while all along reporting our activities to security.

After a while these guys they sent in started causing all sorts of trouble, provoking arguments during the meetings and sowing dissension among us."

"Yeah," yells Woody, "the motherfuckers were provocateurs! They got everybody fighting with each other and pretty soon the whole thing fell apart. It was a mess."

Woody Jakes has never been afraid of expressing himself. His bright red hair and fierce blue eyes are the first things you notice about him. He's Irish American and seems to always be complaining about one thing or another. Today he's talking about the weather. Yesterday it was politics, and the day before he was telling everyone on the ward that he hadn't had a bowel movement in a week.

Woody joined the United States Army right out of high school, the same day his Selective Service Order to report for induction arrived in the mail. He went over to the US Army recruiting office in downtown Birmingham, Alabama, and signed up. Woody didn't want to go into the army, and he didn't want to go to Vietnam, but like many back then, he didn't think he had any other options. Several people he knew from high school had already been killed in the war, and one guy who Woody ran track with had lost both his legs after being "in country" just two weeks.

Woody's a quadriplegic. He tripped a land mine—a "Bouncing Betty" I think they call it—and got his testicles blown apart, not to mention the paralysis of most of his body. He jokes about the testicle part, telling anyone who will listen that it really doesn't matter because he can't use his penis anymore anyway. "If they can't take a joke, fuck 'em!" is by far his favorite line and he uses it a lot.

Woody's father was a World War II veteran and was part of the initial landing force on D-day. Woody doesn't talk about his father much, but he did once show me a picture of his dad smiling and holding his M1 Garand rifle that was taken a week before he died on Omaha Beach. One of his father's buddies had sent it to his mother with a letter Woody said he never read.

Later that afternoon we visit Marty and Willy Jefferson on C ward, and the blind vet Tony D. over on K ward, telling them about our meeting at the senator's office.

I look forward to getting Tony D. to join us, he's someone who will be a strong and respected voice in the AVM. He's an intellectual, a wise and thoughtful man. He always seems to have a book in his hands. The day we visit him and the others he is reading *Siddhartha* by Herman Hesse and says he plans to read *The Stranger* by Albert Camus next. In his pack there are several other braille books, including Bertrand Russell's *A History of Western Philosophy*. He hopes to become a philosophy professor someday.

Tony D. was wounded on the night of June 16, 1966, during Operation Kansas, when a Vietcong grenade blew up in his face, blinding him for life. He doesn't talk about it much, but from what I've heard he saved the lives of several of his men that night and was awarded the Purple Heart and the Navy Cross, one of the highest decorations in the United States Marine Corps. Tony D. was medevaced to the Da Nang intensive care ward and then sent to the Yokosuka Naval Hospital in Japan. He did his rehabilitation at the Central Blind Rehabilitation Center at the Hines VA Hospital in Illinois, where he learned the many skills he would need as a sightless veteran.

Tony is particularly proud of his new braille watch. With one sweep of his fingers across the face of the dial he can tell you the time. It was given to him as a present by his parents when he left Chicago for California, where he moved because of the weather, and to continue his rehab at the Long Beach VA.

I met him for the first time at one of our Patients'/ Workers' Rights Committee meetings. I remember the night he came down, led by one of the other patients, in his blue hospital pajamas and dark sunglasses. He was very quiet at first but after a while he began to talk. He spoke softly and thoughtfully and it was obvious he was very well read. I could tell he cared about us and we immediately accepted him as one of our brothers.

After our talk with Marty, Willy, and Tony D., Bobby and I discuss some of the others we can call. Bobby says Sharon will join us and that his brother Charlie, who just got out of the navy the week before, is interested too. We then decide to phone Joe Hayward, his

wife Annie, and their friend Eddie Campos in Laguna
Beach to see if they are interested as well.

You'd never know it by Joe Hayward's wild, curly red
hair and completely disheveled appearance that his
father was a Marine Corps drill instructor. Joe looks
more like a homeless skid-row veteran than a highly
decorated former marine who served two tours of duty
in Vietnam.

Born and raised at the USMC base at Camp Pendleton in California, Joe grew up in a very strict family. His
father held inspections every morning, making sure
he and his brothers had spit-shined their shoes and
made their beds to exact Marine Corps specifications.
Everything had to be perfect.

When Joe was seventeen his father took him down
to the USMC recruiting office in Oceanside, California, where Joe signed up for the Marine Corps; he
was sent to MCRD San Diego boot camp that spring.
He was promoted to PFC (Private First Class) out of
boot camp which made his father very proud. Several
months later Joe volunteered to go to Vietnam. He par-
ticipated in several operations and was wounded in a
firefight in April of 1968. He was hit by shrapnel from a
Vietcong "Chicom" grenade that shattered his left leg.
He now walks with a permanent limp with the aid of a
cane. It is sort of a hobbling type of walk. He also took
some shrapnel in the face, leaving a permanent scar
just below his left eye.

We met for the first time at an antiwar demon-

stration in downtown LA. Nearly one thousand protesters had shown up that day. Joe and I were part of
the VVAW contingent. There were thirty of us in our
green utility jackets and floppy bush hats, our medals
and ribbons from the war dangling from our chests.

Joe was hard to miss, with his Marine Corp drill instructor's campaign hat tilted contemptuously back on
his head, his ragged USMC utility jacket covered with
his medals, and carrying a bright blue and yellow NLF
(National Liberation Front) flag on a wooden pole. He
claimed to have become a revolutionary, radicalized
when he was arrested and beaten by police during a
demonstration at Saddleback College not long after
returning from Vietnam.

I was well aware of the fact that quite a few people in the antiwar movement supported the NLF, my
former girlfriend Carol being one of them. A familiar
chant of the day had been, "Hey hey! Ho Chi Minh!
NLF is gonna win!" And it was also quite common for
protesters to wear rings and bracelets made from the
wreckage of American B-52 bombers shot down by
the North Vietnamese. This seemed to be a source of
great pride for them, not to mention a status symbol
in the movement. Carol once said she was proud to
wear the ring from an American fighter plane that had
been shot down, angrily telling me the pilots were all
murderers and war criminals and were killing innocent
Vietnamese children.

Though I knew I could never wear that ring, I
could certainly understand why Carol and the others

felt the way they did. I strongly sympathized with the Vietnamese people and the absolute terror they must have been experiencing every day as we continued to drop more bombs on them than all the bombs dropped during World War II. Millions of men, women, and children had been killed, and I couldn't help but wonder if the pilots flying those missions ever thought of all the human suffering they were causing, or if Carol and the others in the movement wearing those rings ever thought of the pilots who had died.

Joe is a mix of contradictions. He is deeply cynical and sarcastic, but when he calls you *brother* you know he really means it. There is an anger churning deep within him. He speaks very softly, appearing easygoing and polite, but just below the surface there is a seething rage, a powder keg about to explode.

Joe, like me, joined the VVAW not long after Operation Dewey Canyon in 1969. His father completely disowned him, calling him a traitor and refusing to take his phone calls. Joe is hurting inside; he trusts no one and like many of us he seems lost.

Joe and Annie appear to be the perfect couple. Annie is young and beautiful; a true flower child of the seventies who loves to wear granny dresses. She's sexy, sweet, and gentle, while at the same time capable of great loyalty, and she stands up for what she believes in.

Eddie Campos was born in Baltimore, Maryland, in 1947. He joined the Marine Corps out of high school in 1965 and was wounded in an NVA artillery attack on June 11, 1968, during the siege at Khe Sanh. He got hit in his left arm with shrapnel, causing permanent nerve damage.

"The doctors wanted to cut it off," Eddie once said to me with a laugh. "But I told them, *Touch that arm and I'll motherfucking kill you.* I kept my arm." He still suffers from horrific nightmares almost every night. He tells Joe he's afraid to close his eyes, afraid he'll never wake up.

"After I got hit, I lost a lot of blood. It was a heavy artillery attack. We took a lot of rounds," Eddie explained. "There were shells screaming in and exploding all around us. We were in our sandbagged bunker. I thought I was going to die. I was saying my Hail Marys. I just wanted it to fucking stop. Suddenly it became quiet and I ran out of the bunker with my medical bag to see if there was anybody I could help. Men were screaming all around me. One bunker had gotten a direct hit and everyone inside was dead, ripped to bloody shreds by the shrapnel—there was the smell of gunpowder in the air mixed with blood. Then it all started up again and that's when I got hit. The corpsman came and did his best to stop the bleeding. They put me on a chopper and I was thinking, *I've got to stay awake. I can't close my fucking eyes.* There were people screaming all around me and all I could think was that if I closed my eyes I might die."

In many ways Eddie's still very gung ho and continues to act and speak like a marine, using all the familiar Marine Corps lingo. He is extremely disciplined and struts around the SCI ward in his jungle boots and perfectly starched utility jacket, his long black hair reaching all the way down to his waist, barking orders and commands to no one in particular. Eddie is very proud to have been a marine and that is something no one will ever take away from him. "Once a marine, always a marine!" he likes to say, though he has already marched with Joe and Annie in several antiwar demonstrations.

Eddie, like a lot of us, has conflicting feelings about the war. He had been so certain back in '65. He imagined being part of a great victory like his father who had fought in World War II. *It'll all be over quickly*, he thought. But slowly, Eddie came to realize we were not going to win in Vietnam and that was painful and devastating for him. He felt betrayed and couldn't understand why his government had not done all it could to win the war.

"Do they have any idea how much we sacrificed, how many have been killed and maimed? We're gonna lose that fucking war," he mumbled bitterly one morning, soon after he decided to become a volunteer on the SCI ward in Long Beach, wanting to do all he could to help his wounded brothers.

When Bobby and I leave the wards that afternoon, I push my wheelchair into the parking lot where the bright afternoon sunshine hits my face. I can't help but feel like a prisoner who has just escaped from a dark and depressing dungeon. I still hate this place.

It frightens me, yet even as I think this, I know it will only be a matter of time before I'll be back here again. We all know this. We live with this every day. It is the nature of our injuries, of being a paraplegic or a quadriplegic. We will be in and out of this place for as long as we live. That's just the way it is.

I know I will have nightmares tonight. It's always that way when I come to this place. It will take a day or two to shake all this from my mind, but none of that seems to matter right now. Something has changed and I feel a powerful stirring within me.

I take a deep breath of the fresh spring air and look up into the bright blue sky above the hospital. It's a beautiful day, a perfect day. I'm free of this place, at least for now, and the world outside seems so inviting.

Over the next few days we return to the VA, continuing to converse with our friends on the ward, doing our best to convince them to join us on Tuesday for the meeting in Senator Cranston's office. Nick is now definitely with us. Marty's still not sure, and Danny is wavering. Woody, Jafu, and Willy Jefferson say they are committed to coming. Joe, Annie, and Eddie Campos will also be joining us. Tony D. tells me he will do his best to take part. In the end, eleven agree to join us at the senator's office.

Even though everything seems to be coming together, I'm still concerned. There are just too many things that can go wrong. We need to have better control of the situation if we intend to have it all go

smoothly, and it *must* go smoothly. I know some of them
might change their minds. Don't ask me how I know,
I just do. I've been on those wards in the early morning
and I know what it's like. They wake you up really early,
usually a little after six. They take your blood pressure
and temperature. You're still half-awake and some guy
comes in a few minutes later to draw your blood. He
leaves and you try to go back to sleep, but just as you
begin to close your eyes the nurse comes in to give you
your pills. At seven a.m. a guy from the food services
department arrives and places a tray with your breakfast on the table next to your bed. Most of the guys
don't eat their breakfast, they just sleep. A lot of them
have hangovers from all the drinking and drugs they
did the night before. They don't want to deal with the
morning. They feel defeated, beaten down. Marty has
already attempted suicide twice this year. Nick keeps
complaining that if things don't improve he's going to
blow his brains out. A lot of them sleep until noon. I
can only imagine how difficult it will be trying to get
them all up and out of the wards for the trip to Senator
Cranston's office in Westwood.

Finally, Bobby and I settle on a new plan.

"We've got to get everyone over to your place by
Monday night. That's the only way this thing is going
to work," I tell Bobby. His apartment is in Long Beach,
only a few miles from the hospital. "They can all sleep
there Monday night and we'll leave for Cranston's office in the morning around eleven to make it in time
for the two o'clock meeting."

We tell everyone that Bobby's wife Sharon plans to cook a delicious meal. That seems to help, and somehow, by that Monday afternoon, we are able to get all of them off the wards and over to Bobby and Sharon's apartment. We use three cars, with Joe, Eddie, and Bobby doing the driving. For the most part everything goes smoothly.

# The Last Supper

*February 11, 1974*

Sharon cooks a spaghetti dinner on Monday night, with Bobby dishing out large portions to everyone.

"This is delicious, Sharon!" I shout.

Bobby makes everyone feel comfortable and welcome. "Don't worry, we've got plenty of room," he says. "Sharon and I will sleep on an air mattress here in the living room. Danny and Woody can have our bed. The rest of you guys can sleep on the mattresses on the floor."

After dinner, when everyone has been transferred onto their mattresses, we carefully go over the plans for the next day, explaining how we will be convoying in several cars over to the Federal Building in Westwood. I explain how everyone is to wear his uniform with ribbons and medals. We want to make a good impression at the meeting.

I look at them that night sprawled out on the living room floor. Willy Jefferson is telling everyone about his son. He's got an old, faded photo he's passing around the room. Nick is entertaining Annie in the kitchen with his dummy, Edgar. Nick is very good and the dummy is making Annie laugh. Danny, who is paralyzed from the neck down, insists that he be propped up on the couch in a sitting position, his lifeless arms dangling by his side.

Tony D. sits alone in the corner playing his guitar. Marty, Woody, and Jafu rest on their mattresses while Joe and Eddie sit on the couch next to Danny, playing cards. It is a peaceful night and our bellies are full from Sharon's spaghetti dinner. I am amazed as I look around the room at all of them. I would never have believed a week ago that we could pull this off, but here we are. Everyone is together, all of us, just the way I had hoped it would be.

I know that I have not been completely honest with them and have purposely withheld information regarding tomorrow's meeting. I am hoping that if I can just get them down there, everything will fall into place. I'm also convinced that if I tell them the whole truth, few, if any of them, will want to go. This is the only way it can be done. We stay up late that night laughing and joking, finally getting to sleep around one a.m.

# PART II

## THE STRIKE

# Tuesday, February 12, 1974

T he following morning we get up early. Sharon makes a big breakfast of scrambled eggs, toast, sausages, and hot cups of coffee for everyone. The smell is so familiar to me and for a moment I am lost in time. I think of my childhood, big breakfasts my father would make on Sundays after church, reading the comics on the living room rug; a quieter time, a more peaceful time before the war.

No one says anything as we quickly get dressed. Eddie carefully places Tony D.'s Navy Cross on the pocket of his green utility jacket. Nick wants his Purple Heart and Bronze Star to be perfect. Joe Hayward lifts Danny into his wheelchair, lacing up his jungle boots and straightening out his hospital pants. I look around me and cannot help but feel we are heading into battle once again.

Around eleven thirty we get everyone into the cars. Bobby lifts Danny into the front seat of his blue Buick station wagon while I transfer into my car, closing up my wheelchair and pulling it into the backseat.

"Remember, stay close together!" I shout to all of them as I lean out my open window.

We head to the freeway and soon we're driving north, six cars, eleven vets and our supporters, and all the AVM flags, banners, and buttons in the trunk of my Oldsmobile. I am the lead vehicle and the others quickly fall in behind. Just as I expected, the freeway is packed with bumper-to-bumper traffic. I look into the rearview mirror, feeling proud as I ease my car into the slow lane, checking to see if the others are still behind me.

"Beautiful!" I shout to Bobby, who is next to me in the passenger seat. "Everyone's still together. We haven't lost anybody." I smile as I pull back gently on the hand controls, reminded of the VVAW "Last Patrol" convoy to the Republican National Convention in Miami in August of 1972.

We continue heading north toward Westwood. The drive is slow, but I'm not concerned. The important thing is that we all get there together. I look at the other cars around me, the commuters heading off to work, and think how within a few hours they may all be hearing about us on the news. Not since the war has there been a day as important and meaningful as I hope this day will be for us. It takes about half an hour to reach the Wilshire Boulevard exit and I glance once again into my rearview mirror, thrilled that we are still together. I am proud of them all.

It takes a certain skill to keep a convoy together, a discipline and focus that I know we will all need in the days ahead. As we continue along Wilshire Boulevard, we pass the Westwood VA hospital on the right, and to my left, behind a tall fence, is what remains of the old soldiers' home, long since fallen into disrepair. Homeless veterans now lay sprawled in front of its locked gate. Within are the sorrowful reminders of a time long gone by; ramshackle, dilapidated buildings now stand in sharp contrast to what once was.

Established in the late 1800s to care for America's disabled veterans, the old soldiers' home once thrived as a vibrant community; an atmosphere of healing, camaraderie, and support prevailed. In the beginning, there were beautiful, spacious lawns, comfortable and well-kept domiciliaries, a chapel, a theater, and even a streetcar depot right on the property. Wounded Civil War veterans and disabled soldiers from World War I were some of its earliest residents. My grandfather James Lamb served with the American Expeditionary Forces in World War I where he was shell-shocked and gassed and, from what my grandmother told me, was never the same again.

We reach the Federal Building at 11000 Wilshire Boulevard. It is a beautiful morning and the bright sunshine sparkles off the great building. We make a sharp right-hand turn at the light on Veterans Avenue, then another quick right into the Federal Building parking lot.

We have made it! We have somehow stayed together even with all the crazy traffic.

I pull into the handicapped parking space, turning

off the engine of the Oldsmobile. All the others are parking now around me and getting out of their cars. Joe is helping Nick into his chair while Bobby's brother Charlie and Sharon are carefully lifting Danny out of the front seat of Charlie's station wagon. I can see Jafu directly in back of me now, using his powerful arms to drag his body across the front seat of his Chevy as Eddie stands by, wanting to assist, but the ex-marine is very stubborn and refuses to allow anyone to help. I look at my watch. It is exactly 1:45 p.m. We have to hurry. Like Jafu, I insist on pushing my wheelchair out of the backseat and onto the ground myself; I open it up, carefully place my cushion on the seat, and then in one quick motion transfer into my chair.

Bobby and I look at each other.

"Let's go!" I say, my heart pounding in my chest. We have assembled everyone in the parking lot and now we head toward the entrance of the building.

Federal employees carrying briefcases hurry past to another day at work, serious-looking men in suits and ties, smartly dressed women; a very straight-looking blonde in a short tight skirt and high heels catches my eye. We are quite a sight. In go the living dead of the Long Beach VA. In they go in their wheelchairs with their withered legs, in their jungle fatigues and boots and rumpled oversize hospital pants. Nick complains. Woody jokes. We enter the building wheeling past a smiling security guard and take the elevator to the thirteenth floor with no one saying a word. The elevator door opens and we head down the hallway. I lead the way, pushing my wheelchair quickly toward Senator Cranston's office. I hesitate for a moment, then head in with the others following behind me.

We are immediately greeted by a secretary in her early twenties sitting behind the reception desk. "Can I help you?" she asks politely.

"My name is Ron Kovic and I'm a Vietnam veteran," I tell her. "And we have a meeting with Senator Cranston today at two o'clock. We came all the way up here from the Long Beach VA. We're Vietnam veterans!" I repeat, sounding very impatient, glancing down at my watch.

The young woman seems a bit perplexed as more and more wheelchairs roll through the door. "Would you just wait one second, please?" she says, picking up the phone.

A few minutes later, a young man—early twenties, well-dressed, button-down collegiate look—walks in. He says his name is Tom Wilkins and that he is one of the senator's aides. I can tell by his voice that he's the same person I spoke to on the phone the week before.

"It's getting a bit crowded in here. Do you think it would be possible for us to move into the other room?" I ask, pointing through an open door which leads into what appears to be a much larger room. "I mean, we've still got paralyzed veterans in wheelchairs out there in the hallway trying to get in. Is it asking too much for you to move us into a larger room?" Then I whisper to Bobby: "We've got to get them into *that* room. The farther we get into the place, the harder it will be for them to throw us out."

I know right away that the tight-fitting waiting area is far too small for us to establish ourselves if we are going to do a sit-in. The senator's aide seems a bit nervous, but in the end he reluctantly agrees, and we file out of the waiting room into the office, with me leading the way. I'm excited that we have gotten this far.

Bobby and Sharon help push Danny and Woody into the room while Charlie positions the wheelchairs so that everybody will feel a part of what is about to happen.

I look around the room at the guys in their wheelchairs—Danny, Marty, Jafu, Willy, Woody, and Nick—their ribbons and medals from the war perfectly aligned on their green utility jackets and hospital shirts; Eddie in his scuffed green jungle boots; Charlie in his navy uniform and sailor's cap, having just recently gotten out of the service; the blind marine vet Tony Dobrinsky, or Tony D. as he likes to be called, with his Silver Star, Purple Heart, and Navy Cross. It's beautiful. Just as I had envisioned it back at the VA when I first told Bobby about my plan. I look again at my watch and see that it is two o'clock.

"We're here for our meeting with Senator Cranston," I say to the aide. "We're here to discuss the disgraceful conditions at the Long Beach VA and VA hospitals all over the country."

"I'm sorry but the senator's not here today," the young man replies.

"Not here? What do you mean he's not here?" I say, almost shouting. "We were specifically told we had a meeting with Senator Cranston here in his office at two o'clock."

"I'm sorry, but there must be some mistake. Senator Cranston's in Washington, DC."

"Washington, DC?" everybody screams at once.

"We came all the way here from the Long Beach Veterans Hospital Spinal Cord Injury ward in our wheelchairs. We're Vietnam veterans and we demand to meet with Senator Cranston. This is outrageous!" I shout.

"Yeah!" Woody cries out. "Where's Senator Cranston? I thought we were supposed to meet with him."

"Fucking bullshit!" yells Eddie.

"As I said on the phone, I'm more than happy to meet with you today," replies the senator's aide, trying to calm everyone down, but we will have none of it.

I give Bobby a thumbs-up to let him know it's time for him to leave the room and start calling the press on the pay phone in the hallway, and time for Charlie to go down to the car and bring up the AVM flags and banner and buttons. Both Nick and I have several AVM flags stuffed under the cushions of our wheelchairs and will take them out as soon as Charlie gets back.

I know we have to act quickly. Within seconds the media will be told that seven paralyzed Vietnam veterans and their supporters have just taken over Senator

Alan Cranston's office and have begun a sit-in. Before we know it the phones will be ringing off the hook, or at least that's my hope. Several minutes pass and then suddenly the phone on the secretary's desk rings in the other room.

"Hello, this is Senator Alan Cranston's office. Can I help you? . . . Yes, yes . . . Well, they are here right now . . . Hold on, please. It's for you," she calls out, seeming a bit puzzled. "It's a reporter from KABC News and he wants to talk to you." She comes in and hands a phone to me and I immediately go into action.

"Hello, this is Ron Kovic of the American Veterans Movement and we've just taken over the office of Senator Alan Cranston here at the Federal Building on Wilshire Boulevard. There are seven of us in wheelchairs—seven paralyzed Vietnam veterans in wheelchairs—and we've begun a sit-in to protest the disgraceful conditions at the Long Beach VA hospital and veterans hospitals all over this country! We are outraged at the way America's veterans are being treated. It's shameful and we demand to meet with Senator Cranston! . . . Yes, that's correct. We have begun a sit-in and we aren't leaving until we meet with the senator!"

"Sit-in?" Danny and Woody look a bit surprised.

The phone rings again.

"It's a reporter from the *Los Angeles Times*!" I shout after the secretary identifies the caller. "You take this one, Nick!"

"What's going on?" Danny asks, shaking his head in

confusion at everything that's happening. "Takeover? Sit-in? Will someone please tell me what the fuck's going on? I thought this was supposed to be a meeting with Senator Cranston and then we were all going out to lunch. Are we still going out to lunch?"

As Danny grows more agitated, Nick has the opposite reaction and starts getting into it. A former child star and an expert at improvisation, he has never shied away from the limelight and a chance to perform; and though he does not yet fully understand everything that is happening around him, he quickly adapts, throwing himself into the unfolding drama.

"That's right," shouts Nick into the phone, "this is the AVM and we've just taken over Senator Cranston's office!"

Soon all the phones in the office seem to be ringing at once. Bobby races back into the room with a big smile on his face, giving me a thumbs-up. Charlie follows quickly behind, carrying the huge, rolled-up, red, white, and blue canvas AVM banner and the box filled with flags and hundreds of AVM buttons.

"ABC News already called and Nick is talking to the *Los Angeles Times* right now," I tell Bobby. "Okay," I say calmly, "let's make sure everyone gets their buttons, and Charlie, would you and Bobby put the AVM banner up over there on the wall above the window?"

Within minutes everyone is proudly wearing their red, white, and blue AVM buttons and have all been handed their official membership cards.

We continue to consolidate our position. Bobby,

Joe, and Annie string up the banner along the side
wall of the senator's office for everyone to see as the
phones keep ringing. Charlie and Eddie begin hanging
the small AVM flags above the door.

"Would someone please tell me what the fuck's
happening?" yells Danny, still confused.

I look around me. It is amazing: Senator Cranston's
office has been transformed into the Veterans' Rights
Hospital Encampment.

"We're going to turn the senator's office into a
veterans hospital for everyone to see!" I shout. "Now
they'll know what's really going on down there at the
VA!" I look at my watch again: it's 2:20. "We demand
to speak with Senator Cranston, and we're not leaving
until we speak with him!" I call out angrily to no one
in particular as the senator's aide, Tom, races back into
the office.

"Look," he says, "I'm trying to get Senator Cranston on the phone right now. He just came out of a
committee meeting and if you can just be patient for a
little while longer, I'm sure we can work this out."

At 2:35 p.m. a reporter and cameraman from KABC
TV arrive. The phones are still ringing and everyone
seems to be talking at once. I'm right in the middle
of briefing the reporter when the senator's aide comes
running into the room again.

"Senator Cranston's on the phone right now and
he wants to speak with you."

I look over at the flashing button on the phone and
then at the KABC reporter and his cameraman. "It's

John Malmin, ©Los Angeles Times

Senator Cranston calling from Washington," I whisper to them. "Make sure you get this."

I grab the phone, squeezing it tightly. "Hello, Senator Cranston? This is Ron Kovic of the American Veterans Movement and we have begun a sit-in in your office today to protest the deplorable conditions at the Long Beach VA hospital. I gave three-quarters of my body in the war and I demand to be treated like a human being! We want the American people to know what's going on in those hospitals, senator. We want them to know the truth that their most seriously wounded veterans are being abused and mistreated! . . . That's right, senator. We demand mattresses, blankets, pillows, sheets. We're going to be spending the night. We will also need hot meals for the men. I've got seven paralyzed veterans in wheelchairs, one blind marine, and several other supporters who are going to need to eat tonight." As I play to the KABC news camera, more interested in the film footage the cameraman is getting than anything the senator is saying, all I can think of is how this is going to look on the evening news.

Amazingly, though the senator does start to get a bit testy a few times, he is able to maintain his calm demeanor through it all, respectfully listening to everything I say. Only once does he admonish me—when I demand that he *immediately* get on a plane and fly out to California and meet with us.

When all is said and done, the senator has agreed to almost all our demands, including the hot meals that he says will be provided by the VA food services department, not to mention the mattresses, blankets, pillows, and sheets which will be forthcoming as well, brought over from the VA hospital in Westwood.

"Thank you, senator," I say politely before hanging up the phone.

I give everyone the thumbs-up. I can't believe our good fortune. Senator Cranston actually called from

Washington, DC, and I spoke to him. In the name of the American Veterans Movement and our sit-in, I made all sorts of wild demands and the senator agreed to most of them. What's more, all of this was filmed by KABC and will be on the evening news. Just as I had predicted to Bobby at the VA cafeteria the week before, when push came to shove the odds were in our favor and Senator Cranston would not oppose us.

For the remainder of that afternoon we continue taking calls from the media. Morale is high and even Danny now seems to be accepting the prospect of spending the night here in the senator's office.

"Don't worry, Danny," I say, "everything's going to be okay. The blankets and mattresses will be here before you know it and tonight we'll have a delicious dinner compliments of Senator Cranston and the United States government!"

Around five o'clock I look down from the thirteenth-floor window at a steady stream of federal employees scurrying toward their cars in the parking lot, heading home. I take a deep breath as a feeling of great satisfaction sweeps over me.

Against all odds, the AVM has established a beachhead. No longer will we be hidden away in their hospitals and told we are crazy for complaining about the way we're being treated. We will be listened to now. I look around me, feeling a sense of pride that's hard to describe. The men, the flags, the banner, the buttons . . . it is no longer just a dream in the trunk of my

Oldsmobile. The AVM has become a reality. We have taken over the senator's office and we are spending the night. Who knows how much further we might be able to take this thing?

# Wednesday, February 13, 1974

The senator's aide, Tom Wilkins, and his secretary, Karen Connelly, arrive early, carefully stepping around the sleeping bodies of the AVM. Somebody turns on the lights and we all start to get up.

"Reveille, reveille!" shouts Bobby Mays in a tired voice. "It's another day at the Veterans' Rights Hospital Encampment, brothers!"

We move slowly this morning. Danny asks Sharon for help emptying his leg bag. Woody, in a groggy voice, complains that his breakfast hasn't arrived yet. I rub the sleep from my eyes as a reporter from the LA *Herald Examiner* walks into the office just as Bobby is helping Danny into his wheelchair.

"Hey! What's for breakfast this morning?" calls Woody, who is now trying to get his pants on.

Sharon is emptying Dan-

**Los Angeles Times**
Feb. 13, 1974

## 15 Veterans Occupy Cranston's Office

Fifteen war veterans, si of them in wheelchair were to spend the night i the Westwood office U.S. Sen. Alan Cransto in protest against "the n; tional disgrace of all Ve

ny's leg bag. "You've got to drink a bit more liquid, Danny. Your urine's a little cloudy this morning."

"All right, all right," Danny whines.

It feels really good to be with all of them. I slept fairly well last night, and I'm feeling very happy. The others seem a bit more upbeat too. There is a comfort in being involved in this fight with people like myself, even if we have no idea where it's headed.

We all wait patiently, hoping for a knock on the door from the Westwood VA food services department, but in the end our breakfast never comes, and by around ten o'clock everything starts to fall apart.

It begins with Marty complaining that he wants to go back to the hospital, that he's not feeling well. "I think my catheter's plugged up. I think I got to have my catheter changed."

"Yeah, I gotta go too," says Woody, making up some excuse about having an appointment that afternoon with his physical therapist. "She's expecting me. I'm really sorry but I gotta go."

Next is Danny: "Is there anybody who can give me a ride back to the hospital? I gotta get back to the hospital. Yesterday you said we'd be back in time for dinner."

One by one they begin to desert.

"You've got to stay! We've got to stay together. We can't give up now," I plead with them. "We're just getting started."

Bobby doesn't know what to do either, I can see

it by the look on his face. He wants to stay and for a while encourages everyone not to give up. "You've got to hang in there, brothers! You can't leave now." But more and more I can see he's caught between wanting to stick to the plan and the fact that he and Sharon are Danny's personal caregivers. And even Bobby's brother Charlie is claiming he has to get back to his apartment in Long Beach to pay his rent and feed his cat. "I thought we were going to come in here, meet with the senator, then go out and have some lunch. I didn't think we'd be spending the night."

"You promised us a meal!" shouts Danny.

"Yeah, I thought it was just going to be for one afternoon," says Marty.

"I never thought I was going to spend the night!" says Joe, grabbing Annie by the hand and walking out the door, with Eddie following quickly behind.

Around one p.m. everyone except for Bobby and I have left, and my dreams of a new organization have vanished. I look around at what remains of the Veterans' Rights Hospital Encampment and our sit-in: the AVM banner is still stretched proudly across the wall and AVM flags, blankets, and mattresses are scattered everywhere.

"Well, it's just you and me now, Bobby," I say, staring into his eyes. "Are you with me, brother, or are you gonna split like all the others?"

Bobby smiles, tilting his head slightly with that *Are you kidding me?* look. We shake hands and I sense at that moment that he's in for the duration. "We will fight, we will win! We're on the side of the AVM!" he shouts with fierceness and a passion that's almost frightening.

Around four o'clock Bobby brings back several candy bars and soft drinks from the hallway vending machine and that is pretty much our breakfast and lunch for the day. The senator's chief of staff, Lou Hastings, walks past without saying a word, while both Karen and Tom smile, acting as if nothing has changed, but I know they understand what's going on—that it is only a matter of time before we leave the office. Yet even with all that certainty of defeat swirling around us, there is some-thing inside me that refuses to surrender, something that knows we must not quit.

As time passes I sense Bobby's mood beginning to change. I can see it coming before he even says any-thing. He seems distant and troubled as he stares out the window.

"Are you okay, Bobby? Are you all right?"

His resolve seems to be slipping. My one ally, the one person I thought I could truly count on. Now he's wavering too, like all the others. Bobby Mays, who had promised to stand by me to the bitter end through thick and thin, who only a few hours before had sworn his loyalty to me and the AVM—"To the death!" he had shouted—was now on the verge of walking out.

I beg him to stay. "Please, Bobby, don't give up now.

I know there are only two of us but we're still here." Yet
no matter how hard I try to convince him, he goes on
and on about how he misses his wife and how he and
Sharon are Danny's caregivers and how if he doesn't
get home right away Danny will probably end up back
in the hospital.

"He needs me!" shouts Bobby, wiping tears from his
eyes.

What can I possibly say to keep him from leaving
me and the AVM from falling completely apart? I have
to think of something quick, even make something up
if I have to. "Look, Bobby," I say, "I'm going to begin a
hunger strike to the death, and if you want to join me,
you can."

Bobby's eyes light up.

"That's right, Bobby, a hunger strike to the death.
We're going to demand to meet with the head of the
VA in Washington, Donald Johnson, and we're going
to refuse to eat a thing until he agrees to meet with
us!"

Maybe it's an act of desperation. Maybe it's simply
that I have nothing left to lose, but even as I say these
words I know that I have stepped over a line where
there will be no going back, no return to things as they
once were.

For a moment, Bobby looks at me and I can see
a strange stirring in his eyes that I have seen before.
This is something he can relate to, something crazy
and dangerous, something completely out of the ordinary and insane, and if there is anything Bobby Charles

Mays hates, it is the ordinary, the normal, *the safe bet*,
the routine.

Born on the same day the Civil War ended (as he's
always telling me), Bobby—a military brat and proud
of it—has always had a fierce hatred for authority.
Whether it was his wild and reckless motorcycle rides
along the Ohio River or his numerous run-ins with the
law, he loves to take risks even if he has no idea what
he's getting into; he would, as people say, leap first and
ask questions later, which is probably the reason he's
gotten into so much trouble all his life.

Without saying a word, Bobby reaches over and
grabs my hand, shaking it then hugging me tightly. He
has made his decision. There will be no turning back
now.

We have made a commitment. It is now life and
death, and I believe both of us know this. There is silence and then we begin to cry. We will escalate our
tactics, and our bodies will now become our weapons.

It is nearly ten p.m. when I call the City News Service and read our press statement to the reporter: *"Two
Vietnam veterans are beginning a hunger strike to the death
in Senator Alan Cranston's office, and we will not end our
strike until the head of the VA, Donald Johnson, agrees to
meet with us."*

I make it clear to the reporter that we are willing to
die for what we believe in. "Just as we were willing to
die in Vietnam," I say as my voice begins to crack. "We
deserve to be treated with respect. We demand to be

treated like human beings! This is a national veterans crisis and we demand an investigation of all VA hospitals nationwide immediately!"

There is no mention of the fact that the rest of the organization abandoned us earlier that day and that there are now only two members remaining in the office. I am convinced that the dramatic impact of two Vietnam veterans vowing to go on a hunger strike to the death in Senator Cranston's office will override our dwindling numbers.

"Good luck to you guys," the reporter says, sounding very grim. "Let us know if there are any further developments."

After wiping more tears from our eyes, Bobby and I hug each other one last time before going to sleep. We have made our decision: two soldiers in the night have sworn a sacred oath; for better or worse, the American Veterans Movement's hunger strike has begun.

# Thursday, February 14, 1974

B obby and I sleep for a few hours that night, and
by six a.m. the phones are ringing off the hook.
Before we have time to realize what's happening, two local TV news crews burst through the senator's door wanting an interview. It's all over the wires
that two Vietnam veterans are on a hunger strike to
the death in Senator Cranston's office.

"That's correct," I say as the cameras begin to roll.
"We have begun a hunger strike to protest the poor
and inhumane treatment of Vietnam veterans at the
Long Beach VA and in VA hospitals all over the country. This is a national veterans crisis. This is a matter of
life and death."

Bobby and I do interviews for most of the morning as camera crews and reporters from different news
outlets around the city continue to call and show up
at the office.

Tom Wilkins and Karen Connelly do their best to
work around us. Tom is frustrated, and has a look on his
face that seems to say, *I can't believe this is happening. Will
things ever get back to normal again after all this craziness?*

At nine thirty, Lou Hastings walks briskly into the office chomping on a big cigar. "Just another day," he says as he heads over to Karen's desk, picks up a pile of papers, and just as quickly walks back toward his private office, carefully stepping over the mattresses and pillows still scattered across the floor.

A reporter from KNX radio asks me where the other veterans are who were here yesterday.

"They're just taking a break. They'll be back in a while," I reply, wondering how much longer I can cover for them and hide the fact that they have all abandoned us. I don't know what else to say so I keep stalling for time. "This is a hunger strike to the death!" I shout.

"How long are you guys planning to go without food? Are you really willing to die for what you believe in?" asks the reporter.

By four o'clock that afternoon most of the press have left and Bobby goes out to one of the vending machines in the hallway to get something to drink. We haven't had any food all day; the last time either of us ate anything was Wednesday afternoon when we had those candy bars.

"Dinner is served," Bobby announces as he comes waltzing through the door with a big smile on his face, carrying two cans of Coke in his hands. I sip mine slowly as I look around the room. Bobby has straightened up the office, making it a bit more presentable, folding all the sheets and blankets and making sure each mattress is in perfect alignment.

\* \* \*

Sometime around six thirty that evening there's a knock at the door. "It's probably more media," I say to Bobby as the door opens and in comes, of all people, Joe Hayward pushing Nick in his wheelchair, followed in quick succession by Sharon, Danny, Willy Jefferson, Marty, Jafu, Woody, Tony D., and Charlie.

"Eddie and Annie are downstairs. They'll be up in a minute," says Joe.

"I can't believe you all came back."

"We had to come back, brother!" shouts Nick.

"We couldn't leave you guys here all by yourselves! We saw you on television. You're famous!" yells Woody.

"Yeah, you're all over the news," Danny says, clearing his throat.

"I heard about it this morning on KNX radio," says Tony D. with a smile.

"All the news, all the fucking time!" squeaks Marty. "Everybody's talking about it down at the hospital."

Even though I'm happy to see them, a part of me still, if but momentarily, resents the fact that they walked away the day before. But I hold no lasting bitterness for those who returned, and like the parable of the prodigal son, all is quickly forgiven.

"Wait till you see what we got, brother!" shouts Eddie as he enters the office, explaining how he and Joe Hayward got the key to one of the SCI supply rooms and "expropriated" all the medical supplies we might need. "Everything from bed bags, catheters, catheter change kits, rubber gloves—you name it, we got it.

They're all in the trunk of my car," says Eddie with a smile.

I thank him, telling him to hold off bringing the supplies up until later that evening when it's quieter and everyone has left for the day. "How did you get the key to the supply room?" I ask Eddie.

He smiles again and tells me that one of the aides on C ward gave it to him. "We got friends, brother."

"We're all AWOL!" shouts Woody, seeming very proud of himself.

In the end, only Nick says he's sorry for abandoning us, but I tell him not to worry about it and that I'm just happy to have him back.

The phones in the office keep ringing with requests for interviews with the "hunger-striking veterans" as the momentum continues to build. The morale of the AVM has never been higher. Around eight that evening everyone begins to get settled, with Bobby helping Danny set up his "lean-to" and rubber air mattress next to one of the senator's desks while Joe, Eddie, and Annie get busy carrying jars of water from the bathroom down the hallway back into the office.

After things have finally quieted down a bit, we hold an impromptu meeting to discuss our plans. The meeting begins around nine forty-five p.m. with me welcoming everyone back to the Veterans' Rights Hospital Encampment. I go on to explain how Bobby Mays will be chairing the meeting and everyone will get a chance to speak.

Danny is first to raise his voice, announcing that something has to immediately be done regarding personal hygiene, bowel care, catheter changes, and washing up at night.

"We need to get a TV and a radio too," Danny adds.

"I got a radio," says Willy Jefferson.

Sharon says she'll call her sister who lives in Venice and see if she'd be willing to loan us a TV.

"We've got to monitor the news!"

Everyone seems to be asking questions at once.

"How long are we planning to go without food?"

"What about showers?"

"How are we going to wash up?"

"What about my meds?"

I explain that we will wash up in the bathroom down the hall right next to the vending machine. We'll have to use the sink and we'll just do the best we can. Sharon and Bobby agree. The two of them volunteer and are quite familiar with changing catheters and all the other things that will be needed for everyone to feel secure if we are to sustain the strike. This seems to ease some fears.

"We'll try to get some towels and facecloths for everybody," I tell them.

There will be no dinner tonight, no visit from the Westwood VA food services department. Large jars of water, Tang, and Gatorade are brought in.

"Can we drink hot chocolate?" asks Jafu.

Soft drinks and water from the vending machines

in the hallway, and pure liquid broth, I explain, will be the main liquids we drink. "Under no circumstances is solid food allowed. That means no candy bars or cookies." I mention Dr. Martin Luther King Jr.'s fast.

"*Any* liquid?" smiles Bobby, grasping the bottle of tequila in his pocket.

"As long as it's liquid, Bobby, I don't care what you drink," I say, shaking my head, thinking how Gandhi would be rolling over in his grave.

"Does that mean we're going to starve to death?" asks Jefferson, sounding worried.

"Snakes have been known to go without food for up to two years," says Eddie, trying to torment poor Jefferson.

"But I ain't no snake!" he shouts, and everyone laughs.

"Jesus fasted for forty days and forty nights," I remind him, and he seems to respond, lifting his eyebrows and nodding his head up and down. "Peaceful, nonviolent, Gandhian methods. That's the approach we'll use."

"Hopefully we can make people more aware of how veterans are being treated," says Woody in a shaky voice, still seeming a bit unsure of himself and the commitment he's about to make.

"Why do we have to fucking go without food?" shouts Marty. "We've sacrificed enough! Why do we have to suffer more? Haven't we suffered enough?"

"I'll say it again—if any of you want to leave now, you can. We'll get you back to the VA. Charlie will drive you back to the hospital right now, no questions asked."

No one says a thing.

"All right," I remember saying, "let's get ready for the night."

Valiums for spasms are handed out by Sharon, who then begins irrigating Danny's and Woody's catheters and cleaning Marty's bedsore with Betadine Solution and a Q-tip, carefully packing it with sterile gauze.

Bobby makes sure everyone is positioned properly on their egg-crate cushions and all the catheters are hooked up to their bed bags for the night. All the medical supplies that Eddie and Joe expropriated from the SCI supply room at the VA are brought up around eleven forty-five p.m. as the song "Midnight Train to Georgia" plays softly on Willy Jefferson's radio. We sleep peacefully that night, all of us together again.

# Friday, February 15, 1974

The following morning is a wild scene, with mattresses scattered everywhere. Bottles of saline solution dangle from IV poles as Sharon scurries around the room emptying bags filled with urine. I can't help but laugh as I look around me, thinking how crazy it all seems. We have literally transformed Senator Cranston's office into a makeshift VA hospital ward. All the medical supplies that Eddie got are now lined up perfectly along the office windowsill: twenty-four irrigation-solution bottles, eleven boxes of latex rubber gloves, sixty tubes of lubricant for cleaning out our rear ends, six dozen plastic bags to put the crap in, seventeen urine bags or "nighttime drainage bags" as they are called, twenty-six catheter-change kits used to insert the catheters into our penises and inflate the little plastic bulbs inside our bladders, enabling us to urinate without wetting our pants. Several boxes of government diapers have been added for those who are incontinent.

As will be the case every morning for the days to follow, we are awakened by the ringing of phones.

"It's KCBS News, they want to do another story about us," announces Eddie. "They're asking if they can send a crew over around noon."

"Tell them we'll be ready," I respond.

Reporters and camera crews continue to show up, many without warning.

"This story's really taking off. It's getting crazy in here!" shouts Woody. Within moments there's a call from a reporter at KABC asking how long we plan to stay on the hunger strike.

"Until hell freezes over!" shouts Nick.

"I think I just had an accident," says Jefferson, sounding frustrated and embarrassed. "Can somebody please help me? I think I just shit in my pants!"

"Jesus Christ! What's that fucking smell?" says Joe, pinching his nose in disgust.

Bobby runs over to clean up Jefferson as quickly as he can.

"My catheter's leaking!" yells Marty. "I think I got another UTI. I want to get into my wheelchair. Hey, Joe, would you please help me get into my chair? I gotta get ready for my interview with CBS!"

"I need a Valium!" shouts Jefferson in the midst of the chaos.

"Hold on, hold on, Willy, I'll be right with you as soon as I finish putting Danny's super-pubic catheter in," Sharon says, and jokes about having to wipe Marty's rear end last night when he shit in his pants.

"I couldn't fucking help it," whines Marty, seeming ashamed.

\* \* \*

We rush around the office that morning trying to get ready. The song "Magic Bus" by the Who is now playing on the radio and we all start banging to the beat. Lou Hastings comes in around nine o'clock, carefully walking through our encampment, tiptoeing over the bodies scattered on the floor.

"Good morning, Lou," Joe says sarcastically.

Hastings just waves his hand and keeps on walking quickly toward his private office in the back.

Tom Wilkins comes into the room a few minutes later, telling us that Hastings is upset about "the odor now p-p-p-permeating the senator's office." He tries to say this tactfully but it comes out all wrong. "This place is beginning to smell like a hospital," he finally says, his face a bit contorted.

"Well, welcome to the fucking VA, brother!" shouts Eddie with a laugh.

Sharon continues to run around the room from mattress to mattress, providing meds and irrigating catheters, while Willy Jefferson is being interviewed by KCBS in the corner. He's telling the reporter all about the first time he met with his VA case officer not long after he got out of the hospital and how frustrating the experience had been for him. We all listen carefully and I can't help but think back to my own experience.

It was late December of 1968 and I had just gotten out of the Bronx Veterans Hospital and begun classes at Hofstra University on the GI Bill. I was living at my parents' house at the time and I got a call from a guy from the VA telling me that he wanted to meet me to discuss my veteran compensation benefits. We agreed to get together in a parking lot not far from the university. It seemed like an odd place to meet but I went along with the guy. He showed up in a suit and tie and was carrying a large leather briefcase filled with all sorts of papers. He got out of his car and jumped into my front seat and opened up his briefcase. He was talking real fast, telling me all about my injury and the disability benefits I'd be receiving. He seemed to be in a terrible hurry. There was no handshake, no greeting or welcome home. It was all business and obviously he had done this many times before. He rattled off statistics like clockwork.

"Let me see," he said, looking down at his papers. "One hundred percent service-connected, totally disabled, complete loss of bowel and bladder function, injured in combat, gunshot wound, paralysis, T-4 level. Is this correct?" he asked, still staring down at his papers. "It's really quite simple," he went on. "For instance, if a soldier or marine loses an arm or a leg in combat, they might get, if they're lucky, 30 to 40 percent disability, but in your case—that is, those of you who have lost everything: legs, bowel, bladder, sexual organs—you'll be receiving the maximum payment. Unlike the guys who lose fewer body parts—loss of a nose, an ear, a finger—that has to be decided on a case-by-case basis. I know a guy who got 10 percent disability payment for having his pinkie shot off; and a navy corpsman who lost his left ear while trying to save a marine—he got

20 percent, I think. It's crazy. There was a guy who got his pecker shot off in a firefight and they finally concluded that he deserved 75 percent compensation for it. He committed suicide before the first check was delivered." He cleared his throat. "You'll be receiving a monthly disability check for the rest of your life. The first payment will begin shortly. It will be tax-free. You will receive free dental, free hospitalization, free psychological counseling if you need it, and when you die," he said, now glancing up from his papers, "we will pay for your burial at any VA cemetery. You can even be buried at Arlington if you want. Quite a few of our 100 percent service-connected combat veterans are buried there."

I sat in my car in the parking lot for a long time after he left that day, staring out the window as I watched the clouds slowly drift across the Long Island sky.

It is Marty who first comes up with the idea of placing a number on the large window in the center office to represent each day without food, for everyone below to see. There is a brief debate regarding what we will use to place the number on the window.

"Why don't we use a bar of soap?" suggests Danny.

"No, that's not going to work. It's got to be something people can see and that we can wash off each day so we can put a new number on every morning," says Jafu.

"I've got an idea!" says Bobby. "I've got some shaving cream in my ditty bag."

"Shaving cream? Don't you think it's gonna run right down the window?" says Danny.

"No, it'll work. You'll see. It'll stay. I'll show you—it'll be better than soap!" Bobby exclaims, running over to where his little pup tent is set up and grabbing his bag. He hurries back over with a can of Gillette shaving cream in his hand and quickly walks to the center office window. "Watch," he says, confidently lifting the can toward the very top of the window, placing the number 2 in the middle. "You see?"

"Only one problem," says Woody, yawning. "You're going to have to write it on there backward."

"Backward?" says Joe.

"He's right!" shouts Marty. "From down below, the number will be backward for anyone looking up. We have to write all the numbers on the window backward."

"Marty's right," says Eddie.

"Great idea, Marty!" I yell. And soon everybody agrees.

Later that day Sharon's sister Kathy and her husband Ed arrive with a small TV and we set it up on a desk in the senator's office. Everyone is excited and looking forward to watching themselves on the news that night. Nick and Joe did interviews earlier in the day with KCBS and KNBC and I did one over the phone with a reporter from KNX radio. I sit listening to the radio, hoping they'll run it, while Woody is talking on the phone to a woman reporter from the *Los Angeles*

*Times* who wants to come down on Sunday and do a feature story about him and the strike.

Around six o'clock we gather around the TV and switch on the local news. A couple hours later the lights are turned out.

It is quiet and I am almost asleep when Willy announces to everyone that tomorrow will be the anniversary of his wounding in the war. It will be exactly six years ago that he was paralyzed in Vietnam. Willy worked in Graves Registration Service, and from what he tells us he had been working with the dead all his life. His father ran a mortuary in Tupelo, Mississippi, where Willy helped out as a boy before he joined the marines.

"I was working with the dead when I was seven," says Willy in his slow Southern drawl. "My dad taught me everything. I should have never told that recruiter that I worked in my dad's mortuary. He wrote something down in my file and the next thing I know, after boot camp they're assigning me to mortuary affairs school in Virginia."

Willy went over to Vietnam in October of '67. He had only been "in country" four months when a Vietcong mortar round made a direct hit on his makeshift mortuary, tearing several corpses to pieces and paralyzing Willy for life. He still has terrible nightmares and not a day goes by that he doesn't think about that experience.

All of us here know the date of our wounding. It is a day none of us can ever forget.

"April 15, 1968," says Marty in a tired voice from under his desk.

"June 16, 1966," mumbles Tony D. softly from across the room.

"June 11, 1968, Khe Sanh," says Eddie proudly as he begins to stand up.

"November 7, 1967!" Woody says in a crackly voice.

"Phu Bai, August 16, 1967," says Sharon firmly. "My brother Tommy died on that day!" She's holding Bobby's hand, squeezing it tightly.

"February 11, 1968, Newport Beach, California!" chimes in Danny, not wanting to be left out. "I got hit by a fucking wave!"

"July 6, 1969, A&J's Liquor Store, Compton, California!" shouts Nick.

"January 20, 1968, Cua Viet, Vietnam," I finally say, biting my lower lip.

# Saturday, February 16, 1974

Today begins the third day of the strike. Bobby is up early, placing the number 3 on the large plate-glass window in the office. He is, of course, drawing it backward so that everyone outside will be able to see that this is our third day without food.

Since it's the weekend, we don't expect much coming and going down below, with most of the offices closed until Monday. It's pretty quiet here. No one from the media has called or come by yet today, and that's a bit unusual considering how intense the coverage has been so far. Normally the phones would be ringing off the hook by now, but I'm not too concerned. Most of the men are busy.

Nick is changing his catheter. He keeps complaining that he can't get it in and eventually has to ask Bobby for help. Sharon is putting a new dressing on Marty Stetson's bedsore while Danny's resting on his mattress. Joe, Tony, and Eddie are filling up our water jars in the men's room in the hallway.

I look at the clock on the wall above me and see

that it's 8:15 a.m. KNBC TV has scheduled an interview at noon and a reporter from the *Los Angeles Times*
Metro section should be coming by around two this
afternoon. There was an excellent article in yesterday's *LA Herald Examiner* that had several photos. The
public seems to really be getting behind us and I can
sense a groundswell of support beginning to develop.
Some of the comments in yesterday's *Examiner* story
by everyday citizens, several of them veterans, were
very positive. There was an exception, though. One
woman, a housewife from Van Nuys, whose husband
is now on his second tour in Vietnam with the 101st
Airborne Division, said she thinks we're going about
things the wrong way and "doing a disservice to those
still fighting and dying." Regardless, the strike seems
to have already evoked a strong emotional response
from the public and I have a feeling this is only the
beginning.

Most of us appear to be adjusting well to the strike.
Woody, however, complained this morning that he
couldn't sleep last night, while Marty told Tony D.
he was feeling weak and was having second thoughts
about continuing on.

Even Sharon admits she isn't sure if we're doing
the right thing and maybe a "less extreme" approach
would be better. I immediately call a meeting in the
center office, defending the hunger strike and telling
everyone that it is by far the best approach and that if
we want to win, we must stick together.

"We've got to be disciplined, brothers! Some of you

might be feeling weak and unsure right now and that's completely normal." I go on to explain that their discomfort will only be temporary, trying not to show that I am also doubtful.

When Bobby and I began the strike three days ago, I wasn't really sure what I was getting into. I knew if I didn't do something quickly everything would fall apart, and Bobby was on the verge of abandoning me. I chose the hunger strike as a tactic because I knew it would be dramatic and hopefully bring us attention. It was a desperate move, but what could I do?

When I first began the fast, I was frightened of what might happen if I continued to go without food. I didn't want to die regardless of how much I tried to convince the press and the others that I was willing to lose my life for what I believed in. That was all show, a way to manipulate the media into covering the strike and get our point across. The truth is, even as I bluster to the press each day about being willing to die for my beliefs, just as I had been willing to die in Vietnam, another part of me is feeling weak, anxious, and afraid. I hadn't expected the others to come back. I'd been surprised when they did. And in those first few days, I'd been worried about the fact that I was risking my health and the health of others around me. Granted, a part of me *was* willing to sacrifice myself for a cause I believed in, but at the same time I knew deep in my heart that I wanted to live.

But now, the initial anxiety over going without food is slowly being replaced by a feeling of calm and a sense of purpose. The changes are very subtle but I am definitely beginning to feel them. I am not as nervous and think about food less and less. I don't really feel hungry anymore. My body seems to be adjusting. My commitment to the hunger strike grows with each passing day. I feel stronger, less afraid. I'm finally beginning to truly believe in what I'm doing and saying. Some of the others have expressed similar feelings.

What is really great is watching someone like Danny, who had been really shy at first about doing interviews, come into his own, speaking much more confidently, almost enjoying expressing himself. And Willy Jefferson, who only a few months before had talked about wanting to die, has suddenly come alive. It's as if we're beginning to discover a whole new side to ourselves and it's an empowering feeling.

In the hospital, we felt weak and afraid, but here in this office we are beginning to discover that we are no longer alone, no longer victims. Almost everyone is really getting into the strike and growing more and more confident, more aware of the impact we're making.

I see those looks of resignation and defeat slowly fading, replaced by sparkles in their eyes. We might be paralyzed and confined to wheelchairs for the rest of our lives, but we have discovered a sense of pride and self-worth we haven't felt since being injured. And as I have felt myself change, I have seen with my own eyes the transformative power of our willingness to risk our lives for what we believe in.

\* \* \*

That evening Sharon and Bobby offer massages to any of the hunger strikers who might need one. Bobby has also recommended some deep-breathing exercises that he says will help people relax.

# Sunday, February 17, 1974

Lynyrd Skynyrd's song "Free Bird" blasts on the radio as Danny asks Joe and Tony D. to help him into his chair. Everyone is getting up slowly. Joe and Tony D. are fixing Danny's pants the way he likes them. Bobby's brother Charlie says that Danny is driving him crazy with all his requests.

"Can you just straighten me up a bit in the chair, brother?" Danny asks. "That's right, just lift me up a little. That's right, Charlie, a little to the left, and could you please pull my pants up just a little more in the back and make sure there are no creases? Now center me on my cushion and pull my pants up a bit more in the back. I'm not sitting on any buttons, am I? Make sure I'm not sitting on any buttons. Just pull my pants up a bit more in the back and—no, no, not like that."

Danny is very demanding and precise in a quiet way, but who can blame him? For a man who has lost everything from the neck down, he has become a superb and seasoned diplomat, a man with nothing but a head issuing orders with the patience and politeness of a priest. Danny knows he must be this way if he is to survive, and both Joe and Tony D. seem to sense this and are in full compliance with his wishes on this Sunday morning. All of us have learned to be that way, and just like Danny, despite our paralyzed bodies, we have all become excellent diplomats.

Danny Prince was paralyzed from the neck down in a surfing accident the week he got out of the air force. He survived a year in Vietnam only to end up paralyzed for life by a fucking wave!

Danny is the most seriously injured of us all. He speaks in a voice that is barely audible. It is best described as a sort of hissing sound that originates deep within his chest as he struggles with great effort to push out the words. Danny makes us all feel lucky. He has lost almost everything; he is nothing but a head.

Danny was sent to Vietnam in August of '66 and was stationed just south of Pleiku where he was assigned a cushy job in the rear, typing up memos, filing reports—a paper pusher, or "office poggie" as we called it in the marines. And though his battalion area was hit by mortars from time to time and he occasionally stood perimeter guard duty, for the most part he saw little action.

He once told me that the toughest part of being in Vietnam for him was the homesickness. "All I thought about all day long was getting back to Newport Beach and surfing. I dreamed about it all the time."

Danny has not let losing everything from his neck

down stop him. He is still very upbeat and reads constantly, anything he can get his hands on: the *Wall Street Journal*, the *New York Times*, *Reader's Digest*, other newspapers, books, even *MAD* magazine. He's got a stack of them. Danny's extremely bright and aware of what's happening in the world. He may have lost most of his body but his mind is still very sharp. He has an amazing memory and can quote everything from history books he's read, to baseball scores, to the latest stock market reports.

What is so remarkable about Danny is that he continues to be very positive, afraid that if for one moment he is negative, everything will all come crashing down. He is clearly aware of his great vulnerability and need of others in order to survive. We all love Danny and accept him as one of our most cherished brothers and do all we can to assist him.

Bobby and Sharon have been his caregivers since they came out to the West Coast in the summer of '73. Without them Danny would still be in the hospital. Unlike Jafu, he doesn't think he will ever walk again. He knows his injury is permanent and is trying to make the best of it.

# Monday, February 18, 1974

Today is the fifth day of the strike and it's the blind Marine Corps veteran Tony D.'s turn to put the number 5 on the window. Soon everyone will be pulling into the parking lot and streaming into the Federal Building. Eddie helps Tony D. as he struggles with the can of shaving cream to write the number.

"I can do it!" says Tony D. stubbornly.

Eddie gently guides his friend's hand in the fluid sweeping motion of a great artist until the backward 5 appears on the window. "Perfect," he tells Tony, who smiles approvingly.

Throughout the morning we take phone calls. The media coverage continues to be extensive, especially the local news stations, who are showing more and more interest in the story.

Yesterday a reporter from KNBC named Don Harris came by around noon to interview us. I was immediately taken by his kindness and concern for our situation. He spoke with a slight Southern accent and I believe he is a man we can trust. He said he wants to put together a major piece on the strike and promised he would do everything he could to alert the public to the conditions at the VA and plight of America's disabled veterans. He plans to make a trip with his crew down to the SCI wards in Long Beach to see for himself.

Most of the day is spent doing interviews both over the phone and in person, with TV crews and reporters showing up in the office at all hours of the day. Around five o'clock, a student reporter from the UCLA *Daily Bruin* newspaper comes by asking if he can do a story. He wants to spend an entire evening with us sometime this week and says a lot of the students on campus have heard about the strike and are interested in knowing more about what's going on. With tears in his eyes he says that his best friend and UCLA classmate was killed in the war just before Christmas. I tell him that we would be happy to have him join us any day and will do everything possible to accommodate him and his newspaper. We agree to get together again Wednesday afternoon.

That night we have our meeting around nine o'clock, and afterward, just before we go to sleep, Eddie tells us he hasn't had any nightmares since the strike began and seems to be sleeping better at night. Up until now, no one has talked that much about the war; even in the interviews that have been done so far we have mostly focused on our treatment in the VA hospital, with little to no mention of our combat experiences.

Eddie, like many of us here, has been plagued by

nightmares and anxiety attacks ever since he came home from Vietnam. I have continued to experience these myself, not to mention the insomnia that has often left me exhausted and barely able to function.

Years from now they will call it PTSD, but for the time being it is something we still do not fully understand. Many of us here are afraid to talk about what we are going through or share with others how anxious and troubled we sometimes feel. It's hard enough being paralyzed from your midchest down without also having to deal with these frightening emotional terrors within.

Someone turns the office lights out at eleven forty-five, and just as we are about to go to sleep I can't help but sense that the day is not over yet, that there are others who wish to say something. Then, out of the darkness . . .

Marty is the first to speak. His voice is quiet, gentle, almost like that of a small child. He talks of the day the men from his platoon came back from patrol with a glass jar. Inside the jar were the fingers and an ear they had cut off a Vietcong solider they had killed. There is silence in the room but everyone is listening.

"Go on, brother," says Tony D. softly.

"I felt sick inside," Marty continues, taking a deep breath. "The men from my platoon were laughing, holding up the jar like it was some kind of trophy, talking about how they were going to bring it home as a souvenir. *What the fuck are we doing over here?* I remember thinking to myself."

Nick is next to speak: "I remember the time I saw a dead Vietcong for the first time. He was killed along the riverbank and he was covered with mud. They dragged the body in a net for the captain to see. We all stood around staring down at him. There were two small bullet holes in his chest. His whole back had been blown out in a shred of blood and guts. Our bullets had turned that Vietnamese boy inside out. I forced myself to not be concerned. *I'm in a war and he's the enemy*, I told myself. The body didn't look human anymore, and I never once thought that body covered with mud could be me someday."

It's getting late but their voices continue . . .

"I thought and daydreamed what it might be like to kill a man," says Woody. "How it would feel to pull the trigger, to take a life out of this world, to blow away another human being, to blow away a gook. *I'll do it*, I thought. *If I have to, I'll do it.*"

"There was this time the captain set fire to a Vietnamese woman's hooch with his Zippo lighter," Willy Jefferson tells us, raising his voice. "She was screaming and crying and had her baby in her arms. I remember how I felt. *This isn't right*, I thought. *We were sent over here to help these people*. But I watched in silence, trying to be a good marine as the woman's hooch burned to the ground, together with everything she owned, because the captain thought she was sympathizing with the enemy," says Jefferson, now beginning to cry.

# Tuesday, February 19, 1974

Someone has put up a large number 6 on the window, and already the press seems to be everywhere. Both KNBC and KCBS are setting up their cameras in the center office and Nick is talking to a guy from the *Los Angeles Times*, who is scribbling down notes in his little pad. There's a woman reporter from the public television station KCET interviewing Danny right now, and several young students and their teacher from a local high school, who walked in just a few minutes ago, are talking to Sharon.

The phones continue to ring almost constantly with requests for interviews, while I struggle to pull myself into my wheelchair. It's nearly twelve noon when I take a call from a guy telling me he's a reporter at the *LA Free Press* and wants to know if he can interview me right now over the phone. I tell him sure, and he begins by asking me how everyone is holding up considering it's our sixth day without any food.

"Pretty good," I tell him. "Most of the guys are adjusting well, but it's not easy." I encourage him to go to the SCI wards in Long Beach. "Go down there and see for yourself what they're going through. It's a slum! It's a national disgrace!"

He then asks me how much longer we're willing to go without food.

"For as long as it takes," I say. "We're ready to die in this place if we have to."

Somebody from D ward called me earlier in the day. I believe it was a friend of Willy Jefferson's and he told me that everybody on the SCI wards has been watching us on TV. "You guys are getting a lot of coverage," he said. "Most of the guys on the ward are with you, but some of the World War II and Korean War vets are really pissed. They're calling you traitors and unpatriotic and saying what you're doing is an insult to all veterans. Ed Callahan, who's head of the Long Beach Veterans Outreach Program, said, *All those guys are Communists and what they're doing is causing a lot of trouble on the paraplegic wards. They're going to give us all a bad name.* Stuff like that. These are the same right-wing vets who criticized you last year when you started the Patients'/Workers' Rights Committee. Now they're attacking you again and condemning the strike."

We all take turns this evening washing up in the hallway bathroom. We normally don't do our sink baths and bowel care until all the federal employees have left for the day. It's better that way, more private. At Parris Island, our drill instructors would curse and scream, telling us it was time to "shit, shower, and shave," and that is exactly what we are doing now.

We sit naked in our wheelchairs running the hot water in the sinks until it rises to the very top. We first clean our private parts—crotch, balls, and penis. You've got to keep your catheter clean. This is very important. You don't want an infection. Next we scrub our faces and wash under our armpits as best we can. We use paper towels and the few VA towels expropriated from the D ward supply room still left.

"These fuckin' towels are getting skanky," says Eddie.

"I'm using my T-shirt!" shouts Marty.

"We gotta get 'em washed," moans Eddie.

"Use the paper towels for now," says Joe.

We brush our teeth with our fingers. It's a bit primitive but we do our best.

"We need to get some fucking toothbrushes and toothpaste in here," complains Woody.

"This will have to do for now," says Tony D., struggling to find the sink. Eddie quickly helps out, gently guiding him.

Joe's wife Annie will be coming up from Laguna Beach this afternoon with some much-needed supplies, and hopefully among them will be the toothbrushes, toothpaste, razors, shaving cream, shampoo, and extra towels that we have requested.

Creedence Clearwater Revival's "Proud Mary" is playing loudly on Jefferson's radio as Sharon and Bob help Marty, taking turns putting on rubber surgical gloves, squeezing gobs of lubricant on the tips of their fingers, then digging deep into Marty's paralyzed rear end, cleaning out all the shit then flushing it down the toilet. They wipe Marty's rear end carefully with a wet paper towel; they know it has to be spotless. Any feces not wiped clean can cause a problem. We, of course, would like to be cleaner, but under the present conditions this is not possible.

Not long after I got out of the Bronx VA, I would often stay at hotels where I had to bathe in the sink due to the fact that back then there were no wheel-in showers. Many of the bathtubs were very difficult, if not impossible, for me to get into, so I'd take off all my clothes in my bed and transfer into my wheelchair, completely naked, filling the sink in the bathroom with hot water. I'd soap myself up good and then, with a wet towel, rinse myself off. I'd dry myself with a towel and transfer back into bed where I would get dressed.

"They used to call it a whore's bath in the marines!" shouts Eddie.

"I had to take a crap in a garbage can one night," says Marty, "in a motel I was staying at, 'cause I couldn't fit my wheelchair into the bathroom all the way. I couldn't reach the toilet so I pissed and shit in the garbage can. I mean, what was I going to do? It was the only motel room available that night so I took it. I just needed a place to sleep. You do what you can with what you got!"

"I can relate, brother," I remember saying to Marty as I flushed my rubber glove down the toilet.

"You're right, brother!" shouts Jefferson, who explains how he's had to empty his piss bag in the gutter or on people's front lawns. "Usually I'd wheel over to a bush or a tree and when no one was looking I'd empty my leg bag, acting as if I was checking out the scenery. Sometimes at night I'd make-believe I was looking up at the stars until all the piss came out and my leg bag was empty. I'd close the clip on the rubber tube at the bottom of it and then be on my merry way. You gotta do what you gotta do, brother," he adds with a smile.

"I pissed on a lot of front tires!" exclaims Marty with a wild laugh.

"Yeah, fuck 'em!" yells Woody. "When my fucking leg bag is full, man, I got to empty it, and if I don't fucking empty it, it's gonna back up into my kidneys and cause autonomic reflux and that can make you really sick."

"Yeah, you don't empty that bag when it's full, you can get reflux and it can kill you, man," agrees Marty. "I heard of a guy who got a ticket for pissing on a fire hydrant."

"You're fucking kidding me!" shouts almost everyone at once.

"It's the truth," Marty says. "He was a para who got so drunk one night his bag grew as hard as a rock. He pissed all over an azalea bush and emptied the rest on a fire hydrant. The cop wrote him a ticket. Public nuisance was the charge and he ended up having to pay a seventy-five-dollar fine."

"Shit," yells Jefferson, "I ain't gonna get no ticket!

When you gotta piss you gotta piss. It ain't my fault they got no bathrooms we can fit into. If I can't find a place to empty my bag, I'm gonna piss wherever I have to and try not to get caught. I mean, you try to be a little discreet, but like I said, when you got to piss, brother, you got to piss—"

"I knew a quad who hooked a long rubber tube to his leg bag," interrupts Marty. "He had to make a long drive and he couldn't get out of his car so his father drilled a hole through the floorboard of his Chevy and stuck the tube through the hole and he pissed all the way to Ohio!"

Everyone laughs.

We finally finish up. It's quite a lengthy process, but by seven thirty p.m. we're done and back in the office again with everyone feeling a little bit better.

Later that night, after the lights are turned out and we're all settled, the conversation that began in the men's room earlier continues.

Joe has some interesting information to share with us. "The senator's got a private bathtub and a shower in his back office," he says, almost matter-of-factly.

"It's first class!" says Eddie.

"Yeah, just like the generals and those congressmen—they got it made," says Marty. "All those senators and top brass get first-class care at Walter Reed. They send us off to the fight their wars and they live like kings in the field, and back home we end up in their rat-infested, stinking VA! Senator Cranston's chief of staff locks the door to that private bathroom every night and here we are out in the hallway bathroom taking a bath in a fucking sink."

We think for a moment of breaking the lock and all taking a bath in the senator's tub, but in the end we decide not to. We know we're fortunate to have gotten this far. We better not push our luck.

# Wednesday, February 20, 1974

These last several days have been amazing. A homeless widow of a Vietnam veteran from Compton showed up in the office yesterday with her son, telling us that she wanted her boy to meet "the brave hunger-striking veterans." *America's finest*, she called us. She went on to tell us that she and her boy were now living in her car. "We don't have much. We took the bus down here soon as we heard about you on the radio. I just had to come and bring my boy."

We were all very touched. Later in the conversation she pulled me aside, telling me that her late husband, a Vietnam veteran named Frank, had committed suicide the year before, after repeated attempts to seek psychiatric help from the VA for his nightmares and anxiety attacks. His requests were denied, the VA claiming they were too backlogged and the only appointment available would be in six months. "He was hurting," she said. "He needed help!"

With tears in her eyes she asked if she could take a photo with us. I said of course, and we all crowded around her and her child in front of the AVM banner.

Eddie took the picture. We thanked them for coming, and I gave her young boy an AVM button and membership card. We hand out membership cards and buttons to everyone who visits, even little kids who come by with their parents—they become honorary members of the AVM.

About an hour or so later an attractive reporter named Elizabeth from a Socialist newspaper showed up. She reminded me of the actress Grace Kelly, and I remember thinking to myself, *What is this beautiful woman doing here?* The paper she wrote for is published weekly and in bright red letters across the front page are the words *THE MILITANT*, and just below, in smaller letters, *A Socialist Newsweekly Published in the Interests of Working People*. I first picked up a copy of the paper a few years ago at an antiwar demonstration. She claimed to be against the war and expressed a fierce hatred for the capitalist system. She proudly told me she was a Trotskyite as she proceeded to take photos of our encampment.

# Los Angeles Times

Feb. 20, 1974

## Protesters in Cranston Office Block Doors to Push Demands

The disabled veterans who have occupied Sen. Alan Cranston's West Los Angeles office for a week will remain there until Donald M. John

statement in Washington saying he will discuss grievances with the group here within 30 days.

Kovic said the veterans will re-

\* \* \*

It's been another long day. After our meeting tonight we all get ready for bed. Sharon and Bobby help lift Danny onto his mattress while Charlie and Joe assist Nick, Willy, and Marty with their transfers. Sharon goes around making sure everyone's catheter is hooked to his bed bag and reminds anyone who needs his catheter irrigated to speak up now.

# Thursday, February 21, 1974

It has been another busy day. It's two thirty p.m. and I've just finished doing an interview with KNX radio. Nick and Danny are in the corner talking to someone from the *Corsair*, the Santa Monica City College newspaper. Eddie stands by the large window in the center office where earlier this morning Marty placed the number. Bobby had to literally lift Marty out of his wheelchair as he leaned against the large plate-glass window and began squirting the shaving cream, creating a nearly perfect number 8. The shaving cream will only last so long before it starts to slowly slide down the window. Right now, it's sort of squashed and sad-looking, but at least for a few hours this morning everyone coming in and out of the Federal Building was able to see it.

Still no word from the VA or anyone in Washington, though we did get an important endorsement this morning from well-respected LA County Supervisor Kenneth (Kenny) Hahn, who has supported veterans in the past. Woody seems to know all about him, having resided in an apartment in Hahn's district and worked on one of his campaigns, claiming that he met him once. He tells us that Hahn served during World War II with the US fleet in the South Pacific, as a commanding officer of a supply ship, and that in 1961 he was the only public official to greet the Reverend Martin Luther King Jr. when he came to Los Angeles after confronting police dogs and water hoses during the civil rights struggle in Birmingham, Alabama. And from what Woody says, Hahn has opposed the war from the very beginning. We are grateful to have his support. We've been calling up various politicians and labor organizations and asking them to send telegrams of support to us here at the office. Once we receive a telegram we immediately alert the press.

Almost time for lights-out. We had a good meeting which ended at nine forty-five p.m. Telegrams of support from both Mayor Tom Bradley and Supervisor Hahn were read aloud to everyone and their words touched us all. Supervisor Hahn reminded us that what we're doing here and what we've been fighting for these past two weeks is making a difference.

Woody says he thinks he's coming down with a bladder infection and Nick complains that his spasms are still bothering him a lot and that he needs more Valium. Sharon has agreed to do an interview tomorrow with the *Kansas City Star*. (The "wife of a Vietnam veteran" story.) She's a little nervous; it will be her first interview, but she's looking forward to it. Up until now, the only other newspapers outside of LA that have covered us have been the *San Francisco Chronicle* and Bobby Mays's favorite publication, the *Berkeley Barb*, but that changed with the call from the *Star* in Kansas City today. I'm hoping that Sharon's interview tomorrow morning will be just the start of more national media covering the story. The press is essential. We need to get more people behind us if we're going to win this strike.

# Friday, February 22, 1974

I 'm up early as we begin the ninth day of our strike. The first bits of early-morning light are just beginning to filter through the open windows of the office, creating a nearly perfect yellow line across the rug where Danny is still sleeping. I open up a can of Diet Coke very carefully, pulling the aluminum pop-top off slowly so as to not make noise and wake any of the others who are still sleeping.

Additional jars of water and packets of Kool-Aid and Tang are distributed by Bobby to all hunger strikers. As I see it, we drink approximately three quarts of Kool-Aid a day, not to mention the coffee, hot chocolate, Dr Pepper, and 7UP we get from the vending machine in the hallway. We are all clearly losing weight and I can see it on our faces. Marty, who was already thin before the strike, has now begun to take on a Christlike appearance. Nick has lost quite a bit of weight. Joe and Eddie seem to be doing okay though Eddie complained that he was feeling short of breath just before he went to bed last night. Woody, who like Marty has always been too thin, seems to be swimming in his oversize hospital pants. Bobby, Danny, Nick, and Charlie are all holding on as best they can, though lately Nick has been complaining of dizzy spells. I'm concerned, but I know we must go on. Sharon had us all laughing when she said that losing a few pounds was something she had wanted to do for quite some time now.

I looked in the mirror at my own face yesterday when I was shaving and I could tell that I'm losing weight too. My cheeks have begun to sink in, but the funny thing is, I feel fine. The craving for food that I felt at the very beginning of the strike seems to have disappeared. It's almost as if eating isn't that important anymore. I've discussed it with Joe and he says he has been experiencing the same thing himself. Jefferson and Woody still joke about eating their imaginary hamburgers, but more and more we all seem to be adjusting.

Tony D. continues to meditate in the corner by the window. He is the most thoughtful and reflective of us all. He is constantly encouraging us with his favorite saying, *Courage does not lie in dying for a cause—dying is only giving. Courage lies in facing the daily daggers of relentless steel and to keep on living.* He says it often and we all now know it by heart. He never complains and likes to quote Shakespeare and Camus frequently. Last night he recited from Henry David Thoreau's essay on civil disobedience and Camus's *The Rebel*.

In many ways Tony D. has become our spiritual guide and inspiration. This man who cannot see has more vision and insight than any of us. He has been at the heart of many of our late-night discussions concerning the war and the hospital and he is not at all hesitant to speak his mind. I do not agree with everything he says, but he definitely makes me think in ways I have not done before.

# Saturday, February 23, 1974

T his morning we receive a surprise visit from the chief surgeon and head of the Spinal Cord Injury Center, Dr. M. He is a familiar face to us all. No one from the hospital sent him here today; he has come on his own.

His expression is one of both compassion and sorrow as he peers across the room at each one of us, "his boys" as he calls us, now camped out on the floor of a United States senator's office.

"Marty, Jafu, Danny, Willy, Ronnie," he says caringly, as if he's reuniting with family; he has dedicated his life to us. He seems sad that it has come to this and that we have had to go to such extremes in order to get our point across.

Dr. M. moves from mattress to mattress checking each one of us: taking our blood pressure, listening to our heartbeats with his stethoscope, checking our pulses. With Sharon's help he cleans Marty's bedsore and packs Willy Jefferson's ulcerated hip with gauze, promising them he will come back again in a few days.

"We are here for you, boys," he says in a voice filled

with compassion. It's the first proper physical exam anyone has given us since we began our hunger strike. We are all touched by his concern.

A few years ago when I was very sick, Dr. M. counseled me at my bedside at the VA, encouraging me to see all the other paralyzed veterans around me as my brothers and telling me that I should continue my education and write history books someday. Often he can be found in the hospital research library. He is forever the student doctor, always eager to learn and grow, to serve everyone, free of prejudice.

Dr. M. is a deeply religious man, a devout Muslim. Born and raised in the slums of Alexandria, Egypt, to a poor family, and having to struggle each day to survive, he somehow graduated from Cairo University School of Medicine at the top of his class. Though many opportunities laid before him, he chose to work among the poorest of the poor: the sick, the blind, and the destitute. He arrived in the United States in 1959 and began working at the Edward Hines, Jr. VA Hospital in Illinois in 1961, eventually being assigned to the Long Beach VA Spinal Cord Injury Center in 1968.

We all understand that Dr. M. is risking his job by coming down here this morning, but none of that seems to matter as he continues to move among us, checking vital signs, bandaging up wounds, and encouraging us. He has taken a sacred oath as a doctor to heal the sick and that is exactly what he's doing on this day. His visit has both inspired me and troubled me at the same time. I'm concerned about what may happen to him if they find out that he has come to visit us.

As I contemplate all that is going on, it is I who now feel guilty for having been so one-sided. In my anger and rage at the VA I failed to take into account that there are others at the hospital like Dr. M. who sincerely care, nurses and aides who feel that same commitment that Dr. M. feels. Even in the midst of all this complexity, things are not so black and white. More than anything I am left humbled by his visit.

Later in the afternoon we all decide to go outside for a bit. The plan is to leave Nick in the office while the rest of us ride the elevator down and go out the entrance of the Federal Building. We feel safe in doing it; we have a fairly friendly relationship with the security guards. Only two days before, Charlie had been allowed to leave the office and go down to get something out of his car after everyone had left for the day and had come back in without any problem.

We take the elevator down to the ground level where we all assemble and wheel past one of the security guards. "We're just going out for a few minutes to get some fresh air," I say to the guy, who just smiles. He seems very friendly and just nods his head.

It's a beautiful afternoon, and the first thing I remember is the sun on my face and how wonderful it felt just to be outside again. We have been cooped up in the office for nearly two weeks and being able to spend even a little bit of time outside comes as a great relief. I remember breathing the fresh spring air as I listened to the hum of traffic on Wilshire Boulevard. All the others sit in their wheelchairs around me.

"We're back in the world again," Tony D. says with a sigh.

"Paradise," says Woody, taking in the view, the green grass and beautiful trees, the birds chirping.

As I sit there, my mind drifts back to my childhood, my youth. I think of the days before the war, before my injury, spring days in Massapequa long ago, our house on Toronto Avenue, the backyard, the trees, my mother and father still so young. Two different worlds, one of innocence and joy, the other of sorrow and despair.

I am so happy to be alive, still alive after all that I've been through, all I've endured, all those agonizing nights and days. Yet even as I celebrate this moment, I can't help but think back to those who did not make it. Cosmo, Briggs, Pat, Al, Pete. I knew them all. It's a long list. It's amazing that I'm still alive when so many others are dead, and at such a young age. Isn't all this dying supposed to happen when you're much older? Not now, not while we're so young. How come the recruiters never mentioned these things? This was never in the slick pamphlets they showed us. This should be a time of innocence, a time of joy and happiness, no cares and youthful dreams—not all these friends dying so young, all this grief and numbness, emptiness and feelings of being so lost.

We all wish the afternoon could last forever but soon it's time to head back to our encampment. I have a funny feeling as we approach the entrance to the Federal Building. I try to push the door open but it won't budge. I push again. "It's locked!" I shout. "They fucking locked us out!"

"Motherfuckers!" yells Eddie. "They're trying to keep us from getting back into the office."

"They want to break the strike. We were set up," says Tony D.

There we are in our wheelchairs with our faces pressed up against the door, locked out. All I can think of is getting back to the senator's office. I can see one of the security guards maybe twenty feet away on the other side of the glass door, smiling and holding out both his hands as if to say, *I can't do anything about it. It's not my problem.*

Without even thinking, we begin banging on the glass door with our fists. Joe joins in, tapping the glass with the handle of his wooden cane. "Let us in! Let us in!" we all shout as Joe keeps banging his cane harder and harder against the glass. "Let us in! Let us in!"

Suddenly there's a terrible shattering sound as the large plate-glass door breaks, and before I know what has happened, Eddie reaches his hand through the broken glass, opens the door, and soon we are pushing our chairs into the main lobby.

"It's not his fault! He had an epileptic fit!" I shout to the security guard.

The guard, to our surprise, pulls his gun out of his holster and points it directly at us.

"You don't want to do that!" I warn as I wheel my chair directly in front of him. "You don't want to shoot me or any of these other people, do you?" I ask, looking him straight in the eyes.

He seems frightened and I can tell he doesn't know what to do.

"We're Vietnam veterans, brother, and we're going upstairs right now. We're going to get on those elevators over there," I state calmly, "and we're going back up to the thirteenth floor to Senator Cranston's office and you're not going to stop us." I look at him one last time, press my lips tightly together, and shout, "Let's go, everyone!"

We all rush forward. We will not be stopped. We did not come this far to be locked out of our Veterans' Rights Hospital Encampment or shot by a security guard. We make it to the elevators, all of us cramming in together. We can't wait to get back to the thirteenth floor. My mind races with all sorts of crazy thoughts. I wonder if we will get in trouble. Will they make us pay for the shattered glass door? What will they tell the press?

We must get back to the office where it's safe, where we will make our stand, where we will do our interviews, where we will drink our liquids from our glass jars, where we will sleep and awaken to another day, and another, until they listen, until we are heard.

Finally the elevator door opens. We've made it. We rush forward with me leading the way. I head straight for Senator Cranston's office, pushing my wheelchair as fast as I can. "You're not going to be-lieve what just happened, Nick!" I shout as I push through the door.

But before I can begin to tell him of our adven-ture, he's already sharing the good news. The CBS Evening News will be covering the strike tonight on national television. He received a tip from a local KCBS reporter.

"The CBS Evening News!" Nick shouts. "We're going to be on national television tonight!" We all cheer—never before has Senator Cranston's office seemed so welcoming and wonderful!

That evening we all crowd around the TV in the center office. We wait patiently for CBS to begin its broadcast. For a moment it seems like the news an-chor might not mention us, then suddenly he starts speaking about the hunger-striking Vietnam veterans in California.

"He's talking about us!" shouts Marty.

"Quiet, quiet!" yells Joe.

The anchor only speaks for a few seconds as ev-eryone around me holds his breath. His words touch us deeply and I remember tears coming to my eyes. Fi-nally we have been recognized. Finally we have broken through and made it onto national television. A great cheer goes up in the room as the anchor concludes the segment.

It is a wonderful feeling. We have finally made it. We have gone national and I think we all feel that we have turned a corner of sorts. *The CBS Evening News,* I say to myself as I wheel back to my mattress. *Now everyone's going to know who we are.*

# Sunday, February 24, 1974

All federal employees are gone for the weekend so it's very quiet this morning. It's my turn today to place the number *11* on the window and I'm looking forward to it. I sit in my wheelchair staring out the large plate-glass window, thinking how much I miss being outside and breathing the fresh air like yesterday. We've been cooped up in this office for nearly two weeks now. The air is stuffy. Danny said the other night that the place is beginning to smell just like the hospital. Joe agreed, saying it stinks like a gym locker. The windows here on the thirteenth floor in Senator Cranston's office are all tightly sealed just like the ones on the paraplegic ward at the VA. The people who work here get to go home every night but we have to breathe the same stuffy air. I'm not complaining. I'm just saying it would be really nice if we could go outside more often and breathe some of that fresh clean air.

Sometime around nine a.m. we receive a call from, of all people, the famous forties film star Ida Lupino. I can't believe it at first when Joe announces that she's on the phone. I've definitely heard of her before but I can't remember a single movie of hers that I've ever seen. Marty knows all about her. She had been a lieutenant in the Women's Ambulance and Defense Corps of America during World War II.

"I'm putting you on speakerphone, Miss Lupino, so all the other guys can hear you! Is that okay with you, Miss Lupino?" I remember Joe shouting.

She is so sincere, telling us all how much she respects what we're doing and how during World War II she had volunteered to work at the famed Hollywood Canteen. "We used to entertain and cook for you boys. We couldn't do enough for you," she says, her voice filled with emotion. She continues speaking almost as if she's lost in time, in another era, talking about the people she met, the boys who never came home, and other famous celebrities like herself who were there.

For the remainder of the day it's fairly quiet, with the exception of a call from Nick's former girlfriend Mona who is now living in Denver, telling Nick she saw him on TV.

# Monday, February 25, 1974

The momentum is definitely beginning to shift! I can feel it this morning. We've already received several phone calls from people around the country who saw the *CBS Evening News* piece. Everyone is very excited. We've called for a press conference this afternoon and are hoping for a large turnout. We spend most of the morning straightening up the office and getting everything ready.

Today is the twelfth day of our strike and we are all holding on as well as we can. Even with all the excitement over making it onto the *CBS Evening News* on Saturday night, we continue to do our best to hide how weak and fragile we have become.

Danny is having problems breathing and Marty keeps complaining that he can't sleep at night. Nick told Sharon that he nearly fainted in the bathroom earlier this morning. Woody continues to urinate blood and Bob and Sharon were irrigating his catheter almost all night; finally, around six this morning, they were able to make it clear. "He's stopped bleeding. It's not even pink anymore. It's as clear as a bell," Bobby tells me.

A student from UCLA called a few minutes ago, asking me if I'd be willing to speak on campus tomorrow around noon. I know I might be taking a chance leaving the office again, but the way I figure it, if I go over to UCLA when they want me to speak, I'll be able to make it back into the Federal Building before it closes. Getting the students' support right now is crucial. I'll bring it up at our meeting tonight, but so far everyone thinks it's a good idea.

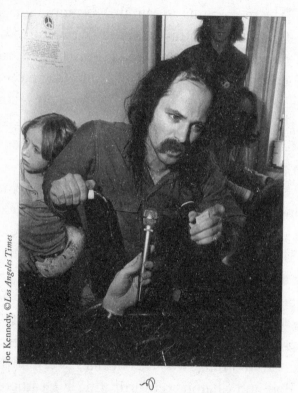

Joe Kennedy, ©*Los Angeles Times*

Around noon we get a call from a reporter from the *New York Times* who has heard of the strike and is writing a column on disabled Vietnam veterans and how they are being treated. He tells us he remembers the *Life* magazine article "Our Forgotten Wounded" in 1970 and wants to see if anything has changed. We put him on speaker and he asks us a few questions. A woman reporter from the *Washington Post* talks to Nick while I do an interview with an independent filmmaker named Michael Harris who tells me he's thinking of making a documentary about our strike.

At twelve forty-five we fill up our water jars and go out to the vending machines in the hallway for some Cokes. The press conference will be starting in a little less than an hour and already several reporters have arrived. I have a feeling we're going to get a lot of coverage today.

Nick collapses during our afternoon press conference. It is really quite a scene, with the paramedics rushing right in during the middle of it all and lifting Nick onto a stretcher. All the networks are filming it. The press is going crazy. Nick appears to be unconscious. His eyes are tightly shut and his left arm keeps twitching. With the cameras still rolling, Joe covers Nick with an American flag, carefully draping it over his body and giving the appearance that Nick is near death. I don't know whether to laugh or cry. It's either one of Nick's greatest performances or he is really in trouble. We're all shouting at once as the paramedics carry him out of the office.

"Hang in there, brother!"

"We're with you, brother!"

"We love you, Nick!"

For the remainder of the afternoon we keep busy taking phone calls and trying to find out how Nick is doing. He's over at the Westwood VA down the street, and last we heard he was on IV and still refusing to eat. Everyone is clearly growing restless and no doubt Nick ending up in the hospital today has only added to our fears and apprehensions.

At night we all crowd around the television as usual to watch the evening news. Several channels—KABC, KNBC, KCBS, and KCAL—cover Nick's collapse during the press conference. The media are running with us and seem to love the story. They make Nick a hero and one channel, I think it was KCAL, has the recorded sound of someone playing "Taps" on a bugle— very dramatic coverage—as the paramedics carry him out on the stretcher with the American flag covering his body. It's extremely moving and I can see that everyone is touched.

The news coverage tonight seems to somehow have united us all again. Around eleven forty-five p.m. someone turns the lights out.

# Tuesday, February 26, 1974

I hardly slept at all last night, maybe two or three hours at most. We plan to issue a press release this morning reiterating our demand that Donald Johnson meet with us here in Senator Cranston's office. We also intend to update the media at that time regarding Nick's medical condition. As of this morning he is still on the intensive care ward at the Westwood VA hospital refusing to eat.

Woody breaks down and cries this afternoon, telling us he doesn't think he can continue the strike. "I'm feeling so weak," he says. "I'm pissing blood again. I got heart palpitations. I just don't know how much longer I can go on."

We tell him that it's okay and that if he wants to end the fast we'll support him all the way.

"Not to worry, brother. You've been one brave motherfucker," Eddie says.

Charlie agrees to drive Woody back to the hospital if he wants. *Who can blame him?* I think. But twenty minutes later Woody tells us he's changed his mind and has decided to stay. "I'm not leaving," the stubborn redheaded Irishman growls. "We will fight and we will win!"

Later that night our contact at the Westwood VA, Dr. Mark Epstein, calls us with an update on Nick: "He still refuses to eat. They're feeding him intravenously. He's asked to see a priest. They're going to give him last rites."

"A priest? Last rites? That son of a bitch!" shouts Willy, his eyes filling with tears.

Suddenly there is silence in the room. In many ways Willy Jefferson's tears speak for all of us. So far we have fought a very brave battle, but we may be reaching the end of our rope. If Nick dies, I don't know what will happen. The strain of all these days—interviews, lack of food, stale air, no baths—seems to be adding up. If things do not change soon I honestly can't say how much longer we can last.

We slowly go back to our mattresses scattered on the floor. It is around eleven p.m. when Joe turns out the lights. For a moment there is complete silence. Then I ask Willy to sing the Lord's Prayer. "I've been singin' that song all my life," Willy has said, telling us his drill instructor at Parris Island had him sing it every night after lights-out. Now, with a bit of coaxing from all of us, he agrees to sing. "*Our Father who art in heaven, hallowed be Thy name . . .*"

Even for those who no longer believe, Willy's voice

is soothing, and in the midst of all this chaos helps to give us strength. We all sleep.

# Wednesday, February 27, 1974

A reporter from the *Los Angeles Times* calls this morning to tell us that Donald Johnson has agreed to meet with us and will be arriving in LA sometime tomorrow. This sudden reversal surprises us all.

"Do you guys have a comment?" the reporter asks from the other end of the phone. "Are you going to end the hunger strike now that Johnson's decided to come? Are you ready to declare victory?"

"Hell no!" shouts Danny. The speakerphone is on so everyone can hear the conversation.

At first I don't know what to say, but soon the words flow quickly. I tell him that we have to meet with Donald Johnson first, and that any decision regarding whether or not we will end the strike has to do with the outcome of the meeting. "I think we've made our demands very clear. We very much appreciate the fact that Mr. Johnson is coming all the way out here from Washington, DC, to meet with us," I say in as conciliatory a tone as possible. "We're looking forward to the meeting and we will definitely be inviting all the press when it occurs."

* * *

It's all over the news, and around six p.m. we crowd around the TV in the center office, excitedly switching from one channel to the next.

"Keep it on channel seven!" shouts Marty.

"Naw, channel two's got better coverage," says Woody.

"Look, there we are!" yells Jefferson.

"And there's Johnson," says Bobby, walking up to the TV screen and pointing to a big picture of the VA chief.

"It's the lead story! Keep it on that channel. Don't change it!" shouts Danny, sounding a bit perturbed.

"Just leave it on one fucking channel," Joe says in a tired voice.

We finally settle on channel two. The woman reporter on TV talks about the reversal of events, beginning with a dramatic film clip of Nick being carried out of the senator's office on the stretcher under the title, *Hunger-Striking Veterans Sense Victory!* This is quickly followed by a photo of a stern-looking Donald Johnson in a suit and tie, horn-rimmed glasses, and the reporter's voice explaining how he has finally agreed to come out and meet with us.

"I can't fucking believe it," says Eddie.

"It's happening, brother," says Joe, shaking his head back and forth. "It's really happening!"

We make up a detailed list of everything from demanding that Johnson resign to calling for an investigation of all VA hospitals nationwide.

"Remember, brothers," Eddie says, "all the fucking media and their uncles are going to be here tomorrow and we better have our shit together. Everything we say and do tomorrow is going to be covered."

There's a lot of kidding and joking around. Everyone seems relieved that the strike might finally be over. All the tension of the last week begins to fade.

"Let's get some fucking sleep, brothers!" shouts Eddie. "Tomorrow's going to come pretty fast and we gotta be ready!"

# Thursday, February 28, 1974

I am up early this morning and notice that Bobby and Eddie are already awake. "Hey, brothers," I say, rubbing my eyes.

"It's a big day, brother," says Bobby, who, with Eddie's help, is moving one of Senator Cranston's desks across the room. "We're setting up for the meeting today."

At around nine o'clock Lou Hastings walks in. Normally he would head straight back to his office without saying a word, but on this day he stops, peering around the room, seeming a bit surprised at all the commotion.

Bobby and Eddie have done their job. The entire middle office has been cleared to make room for the big meeting. Tables, chairs, and several desks have been pushed aside, even our mattresses have been rolled up and placed neatly in a corner, giving the impression that the strike will soon be over. We are excited beyond words. After all these days and nights, all this struggle and frustration, finally we are beginning to sense victory. I am almost afraid to say the word.

\* \* \*

The press begins to show up later in the morning, with local TV stations KABC and KCBS setting up their cameras. A pretty blond reporter from the *Los Angeles Times* clutches tightly to her notepad and pen. The *LA Free Press*, KCET, and KNBC soon arrive. We wait in the office until around noon, the reporters now crowding around us.

Finally the phone rings and someone from the VA regional office says that Mr. Johnson has arrived and is waiting for us in their office down on the seventh floor. I immediately switch to speakerphone.

"Mr. Johnson has arrived," I remember saying loudly so everyone in the press would know what was going on. The KCBS cameraman turns on his camera. "These men have been starving themselves to death for the past fifteen days, many are sick, one of our veterans has already been taken to the hospital!" I shout, telling the guy on the other end of the phone that we are too weak to leave the office and that Donald Johnson must come to us. "Is it asking too much for him to take a thirty-second elevator ride to the thirteenth floor to meet with us? Is Donald Johnson afraid of his own veterans? We demand to meet with Donald Johnson here in our Veterans' Rights Hospital Encampment and we will accept nothing less!"

I don't want to embarrass Mr. Johnson by insisting that he come to us on the thirteenth floor. I know it would be almost as easy for us to go down and meet with him at the VA regional office on the seventh floor, but as far as I'm concerned, it's now a matter of respect. We have gone fifteen days without food, simply asking for a response from the head of the VA, only to be rebuffed time and time again. Nick has already been taken to the hospital. Woody can't last much longer. Jefferson's pissing blood. Marty and Danny are already talking about going back to the VA. It's a miracle that we've been able to keep it together so far. We feel the least he could do after all we've been through is to meet with us in our encampment here on the thirteenth floor.

By now all the cameras are rolling as we wait for an answer, but there's nothing except silence on the other end of the phone. "Are you there? I'm still waiting," I say, pressing my lips tightly together.

Eventually the voice comes back on the line, telling me that he will share my "concerns" with Mr. Johnson and get back to me within a few minutes.

Five minutes pass, then ten, then a half hour, as we begin to realize we're not going to get a callback. At around one, nearly forty minutes after my last contact with the VA representative, a reporter from the Reuters News Agency walks into the senator's office and says that Donald Johnson has just left the Federal Building and is heading back to Washington.

## Los Angeles Times

March 1, 1974

### VA Chief, Veterans Won't Budge; Meeting Called Off

**BY DAVE SMITH**
Times Staff Writer

Donald M. Johnson, national director of the Veterans Administration, made a surprise flight to Los Angeles Thursday to meet with dissent veterans who have occupied

Johnson indicated to newsmen that it might, indeed, be too much "I will meet with them only on V grounds," he said. "In order to ha

"He's running away!" shouts Bobby.

"He's abandoned us!" yells Woody. "He thinks now that he left and has gone back to Washington that we're going to give up and end the strike, but that's not what's going to happen."

"How much more will we have to sacrifice before we're finally listened to?" I remember shouting as the cameras continued to roll.

# Friday, March 1, 1974

The following morning there's a photo on page three of the *Los Angeles Times* of me leaning over in my wheelchair, looking very tired and speaking into one of the reporters' microphones. Joe is sitting in front of me. Woody, with his long, flowing red hair, sits in his wheelchair directly behind me. Next to the photo is a picture of Donald Johnson looking all the bureaucrat with his three-piece suit, horn-rimmed glasses, and American flag pin placed smartly on his lapel. Below both photos is the caption, "STAND-OFF," with an article recounting what happened the day before, with someone likening Johnson's refusal to meet with us to the saying, *If the mountain will not come to Muhammad, then Muhammad must go to the mountain.*

The mood today could not be worse, with no one saying much of anything for a long time. We move around the office like lost souls for most of the afternoon. I hardly slept at all last night and the only interview I do is around one o'clock when a reporter from the Associated Press calls asking if the strike is over. "Absolutely not!" I remember telling him. "Johnson made a big mistake going back to Washington and refusing to meet with us. We demand to meet with Donald Johnson here in Senator Cranston's office and we will not leave until our demands are met!" He keeps pressing me, asking why we refused to go down to the VA regional office to meet with Johnson, suggesting that we may have missed our last chance at a peaceful resolution to the strike, but I remain firm, insisting that we are here to stay and are still willing to die for what we believe in. "We're not leaving until that meeting takes place," I say, hanging up the phone.

We'd come so close yesterday, our hopes and expectations reaching fever pitch, only to have them come crashing down. I try my best to stand by my decision, but the truth is, I'm not sure how much longer we can hold on. Earlier this morning they shut the phones off. Everyone is exhausted. You can see it on their faces and I can now sense a rumbling just below the surface with all the others. Call it my intuition, but something tells me that everything is about to blow.

At seven o'clock we begin our nightly meeting and I can tell from the start there's going to be trouble. Joe Hayward is the first to speak, sounding very frustrated. "We were so fucking close," he says, placing the knuckle of his thumb in his mouth and biting down as he stares at the floor.

"Yeah, we fucking blew it," Eddie sighs bitterly.

"He's not coming back. That was our one fucking chance," mumbles Joe again.

"He had his chance," says Danny.

"He wouldn't take a thirty-second elevator ride to meet with us!" shouts Woody.

Everyone's now talking at once.

"God, we coulda won this thing," says Bobby, suddenly standing up and peering out the window. "Why did we have to be so stubborn?"

"A thirty-second elevator ride. That's all he had to do."

"We came so close and now we got nothing," says Charlie, shaking his head and looking very sad. "He should have come up here."

"Maybe we should have gone down there," says Joe. "We fucked up!"

"What do you mean we fucked up?" yells Bobby.

"We did," says Joe, sounding more sure of himself. "All we had to do was—"

"We made a big mistake," interrupts Eddie. "We should have met with him. It's a fucking shame. We should have gone down to the seventh floor and fucking met with him there. You and I could have met with him."

"We missed our chance," agrees Jafu.

"Yeah, what are we going to do now?" says Woody. "I'm tired of this shit."

"It's over, man!" yells Eddie. "It's fucking over! I haven't had a bath in two fucking weeks. I'm starving! I think we made our fucking point. We did all we could do. I think we should have a vote! All in favor of ending the fucking strike, raise your hands!"

"We can't give up now!" yells Bobby. "*He* made a big mistake, man. I'm telling you, he's going to regret that he ever went back to Washington. People are going to be pissed. I'm telling you, Johnson made a big mistake!"

"I don't know about that," says Danny, clearing his throat. "Maybe Eddie and Joe are right. Maybe we did blow it. Maybe we should just end the strike and declare victory."

Everything seems to be falling apart. Joe, out of sheer frustration, rips one of the AVM flags off the wall, tossing it onto the office floor. This infuriates Bobby Mays, who begins swinging his fist in the air wildly at no one in particular, then slamming it on one of the desks until I'm sure he's going to break his hand.

"Goddamnit!" screams Mays. "We go sixteen fucking days without any food and now you're going to quit? You're nothing but a motherfucking coward," he says, pointing his finger directly at Joe.

Bobby and Joe are now screaming at each other. I can't remember who throws the first punch, but soon both of them are on the floor of the senator's office, punching and screaming.

"You fucking motherfucker! You fucking coward!"

Everybody is yelling as Bobby and Joe keep pounding each other with their fists, punching, clawing, and scratching like two wild animals. Somewhere in the middle of it all, Willy Jefferson's radio gets knocked to the floor. Jefferson begins to cry. Charlie and Eddie finally pull them apart. It's ugly.

"I'm fucking leaving!" shouts Danny. "I want to go back to the hospital. I've had enough of this shit!"

And just as it seems everything is about to fall apart, out of nowhere Nick comes wheeling through the door of Senator Cranston's office, followed by a pretty young blonde in a candy striper's uniform.

"Nick!" I shout, feeling happy and relieved at the same time. "We thought you were dead, brother!"

"Hey, brother, it's so good to have you back," says Bobby. "How are you feeling? When did they let you out?"

Nick's unexpected arrival changes everything. At least for the moment there's peace again, everyone waiting to hear what Nick has to say.

"We've been so worried about you, brother. They said you were in intensive care and you asked the priest to give you last rights!" exclaims Willy Jefferson.

"You fucking freaked us all out, brother," says Woody.

"I'm fine," replies Nick, grabbing ahold of his candy-striper girlfriend's hand and squeezing it tightly. But he can sense something's wrong. He sees the broken radio, the torn AVM flag, the look of distress on all our faces. "What's going on here?"

"It's fucking over, man! The strike's fucking over! We're ending the strike!" yells Woody.

"Ending the strike? Are you crazy? Haven't you heard the news?" says Nick. "We're heroes, brothers!

Where the fuck have you all been? Haven't you heard
the news? Everybody's talking about us. All the aides
and nurses and even some doctors are ready to testify.
There's going to be an investigation. You won't believe
what's happening out there! When Johnson refused to
meet with you guys and flew back to Washington, everybody went fucking crazy! You guys have no idea the
impact you've made. Leaving? Ending the strike? Are
you fucking crazy? It's already on the news. There was
a press conference in Washington this morning and a
journalist asked Nixon, *What about those hunger-striking
Vietnam veterans out in LA? Are you going to let them
starve to death, Mr. President?* He talked about how
Johnson had gone all the way out and wouldn't take
the elevator to the thirteenth floor and then just left
without ever meeting with the veterans in Cranston's
office. It's all over the news. Haven't you heard? Johnson's coming back. Nixon's sending him back to meet
with us and he's going to be here tomorrow morning
and he's going to meet us right here in our encampment! And that's why I had to come. Nothing in the
world would keep me away from my brothers!"

A great cheer goes up in the room and I even notice Lou Hastings's head peek out from his office with
what appears to be a smile on his face. Only moments
before we were on the verge of giving up, and now,
suddenly, we're back together again, as tight as ever.

"We will fight and we will win!" shouts Nick, as everybody starts hugging each other, laughing and danc-
ing right there in the senator's office. Even Danny Prince

and Sharon are doing a little jig, with Sharon holding Danny's hand.

# Saturday, March 2, 1974

I t's hard to believe this day has finally come. We spend the whole morning cleaning up once again. The phones are back on and working perfectly. The press arrives early, filling up every corner of the room. The AP and UPI reporters sit on top of Senator Cranston's desk while a reporter from the Spanish newspaper *La Opinión* stands by the open doorway, his Nikon camera slung around his neck. CBS, ABC, and NBC are setting up their cameras while a short guy from the *LA Daily News* keeps fidgeting with his watch. A reporter from KNX radio wants to do a live interview over the phone and Nick is more than happy to oblige.

Two young student reporters from the radical high school newspaper *Red Tide* show up in their military fatigue jackets and red armbands, asking if they can get a seat right up front. Their history teacher, a Mr. Paterson, accompanies them, explaining to us that everyone at University High, or "Uni" as they call it, is following the strike very closely and it's now being discussed in all his classes. I tell them how proud I am of them.

\* \* \*

I can still remember Donald Johnson walking briskly into the room later that morning in his pin-striped suit, light-blue tie, and American flag lapel pin on his collar. For a moment there is silence, almost as if no one knows what to say, then suddenly we all seem to be shouting at once as seventeen days of pent-up emotions come pouring out.

"What took you so long, Mr. Johnson?"

"When is the VA going to stop abusing its veterans?"

"This is a national veterans crisis! All we're asking is to be treated like human beings!"

"We served this country. We fought for this country! I gave three-quarters of my body in that war!"

Through it all, Johnson maintains his composure.

"Let him speak!" someone shouts from the back as things finally begin to settle down.

"That is untrue," says Johnson calmly. "We have never mistreated our veterans. We provide the highest quality of care for our veterans."

"That's a lie!" shouts Bobby Mays, stepping forward.

"Bullshit!" yells Sharon, standing up. "When was the last time you visited a VA hospital, Mr. Johnson? Do you have any idea what's going on down there? Do you even care?"

"Do not tell me I have no empathy for the veterans of this country," Johnson shoots back. "I fought in World War II. My father died in World War I. My foster father was disabled in that war. My son is a disabled veteran. I am not insensitive to the needs of our veterans."

I remember blocking out everything Johnson said that afternoon, still playing to the media, continuing to press home our demands that I had repeated dozens if not hundreds of times over the past two weeks.

Speaking in a tired voice, I tell Johnson about the overcrowded conditions on the wards and how patients are being abused and neglected. "Veterans are drowning in a sea of VA bureaucracy," I say. "Some have to wait for months before they get the care they deserve." I tell him of the woman from Compton whose husband committed suicide after repeated attempts to seek psychiatric help from the VA for his nightmares and anxiety attacks, the VA claiming they were too backlogged and the only appointment available would be in six months. I speak of the threats and intimidation, the paralyzed veterans who are sent to the psychiatric ward for complaining about the way they're being treated. I remind him of the Bronx VA and the May 1970 *Life* magazine article, "Our Forgotten Wounded."

"I was on that ward, Mr. Johnson." I tell him of the rats, and men left lying in their own excrement, sometimes for hours, pushing call buttons for aides who never come. "How many more veterans are going to have to die before we are finally listened to?" I say as my voice finally gives out.

An hour or so later Johnson leaves, promising to meet with us again within a few weeks, saying that he is impressed with our proposal for reforming the Veterans

Administration, which includes annual inspections of VA hospitals and the establishment of a national hotline to help veterans cut through red tape.

We hold an impromptu press conference in the office, telling the media that the strike is now officially over and that we are leaving Senator Cranston's office for good. We thank the senator's chief of staff Lou Hastings, his secretary Karen Connelly, and his aide Tom Wilkins for their patience and hospitality during the strike, and I distinctly remember a tear coming to Nick's eye when Sharon presented Hastings with a dozen red roses her sister Kathy had brought in earlier that morning. Pieces of celery and carrots are handed out and it's the first bite of solid food I've had in seventeen days. I can still remember the crunching sound as I bit into the celery. We had all joked about who would be the first to break the fast. Joe brags that he could have gone on for weeks more if he'd had to, but soon we are all eating our carrots and celery.

We finally leave the office not long after that, with Bobby pushing my chair into the waiting elevator. We get down to the ground floor and more press is waiting there, clicking their cameras.

We all go back to Hurricane Street and continue the celebration, ordering several large pizzas, swearing that we will stay together forever. We eventually get to sleep sometime around one a.m.

None of us know what the future holds for us or what might become of us in the months and years to come, but there is a comfort in our togetherness on Hurricane Street that night and a feeling that nothing can ever break us apart.

# PART III

## THE AFTERMATH

# Victory!

The following morning there's a front-page story in the *Los Angeles Times* with a photo of Bobby Mays pushing me in my wheelchair out the front door of the Federal Building. In the photo Bobby's fist is raised high in the air and I'm giving the peace sign; underneath is a caption with the words, "End of a Battle."

It is a wonderful day and I feel so proud holding the paper in my hands. Bobby and I buy all the copies we can for the guys, making sure everyone gets one. Everywhere we go that day people are saying hello, shaking our hands, and patting us on the backs. They all know who we are now and it feels great.

We spend most of that afternoon continuing to celebrate, taking calls from all over the city, and even doing an interview with a local TV station that unexpectedly shows up on our doorstep. Late in the afternoon Joe and Annie go down to the beach while Bobby and I head over to the pier; Bobby pushes me out to the very end, where we both sit breathing the fresh sea air, staring out into that vast Pacific, not saying anything for a long time.

It goes on like this for several days until we finally begin to settle into a routine of sorts. There is talk of a reunion, of us getting together in front of the Federal Building every spring to commemorate the strike and hold a press conference, laying a wreath or flowers, making it a tradition. "So people will never forget," says Woody.

Friends and neighbors still drop by from time to time, wanting to say hello, telling us they saw us on TV, and occasionally asking us to sign autographs for their kids. There are a few more interviews here and there but for the most part the intense coverage we received during the strike begins to slowly subside, with things pretty much getting back to normal.

It is a bit of an adjustment at first, with the usual complaints and grumbling that go with no longer being in the spotlight, especially for a bunch of guys who were virtually unknown the month before and had suddenly become front-page news. We continue to hold nightly meetings on Hurricane Street, doing our best to keep everyone's spirits up, reminding them that the AVM is a new organization and that we will have to go through some "growing pains," and just because it has gotten a little quiet and we aren't getting the attention we are used to anymore, we shouldn't get depressed.

"Look," I remember saying, "there's every reason to be optimistic. We've got a bright future ahead of us.

We're just getting started!" But it doesn't seem to help.

"I want to go back to the hospital," Marty announces one morning, and soon everyone seems to be talking about leaving and how maybe we should reconsider staying together forever.

"Maybe it's time we think about our futures!" shouts Nick, talking all about how he plans to get into show business and go on the Johnny Carson show with his dummy Edgar "and become really famous."

Maybe they are right and it's finally time we all go our separate ways, but the thought of breaking up the AVM and ending up alone on Hurricane Street again frightens me. As my dream of the AVM being the catalyst for a great uprising begins to fade, I plead, "We've got to stay together, brothers. We can't quit now!"

Once again I know I have to do something fast if I'm going to keep everyone together, and I immediately suggest an even greater action. And just as I withheld some facts in order to get all the guys to come with me to Senator Cranston's office and launch the sit-in, I begin doing the same thing all over again, refusing to tell them of my hidden agenda, knowing full well that few if any will join me if they know of all I hope to achieve.

It is a wild idea: my plan is to lead a Second American Bonus March of veterans on the nation's capital, where we will demand an even greater commitment from our elected officials to truly address the national veterans crisis in a lasting way. We will organize veterans and everyday citizens from all over the country to join us and march on the White House, just as the veterans in the first Bonus March did in 1932—camping out on the Anacostia Flats and demanding their bonuses.

Hurricane Street once again becomes a beehive of activity. Even some of our neighbors come by to help. It's an exciting time and soon all of us have great expectations. We begin doing interviews again and I start making all sorts of predictions. "We've got commitments from veterans from all over the country," I announce, going a bit overboard. "We're expecting thousands, tens of thousands! They're going to come from everywhere—traveling on buses, cars, trains—just like the Bonus Army back in the thirties. Veteran caravans will be coming from New York, Chicago, Denver, San Francisco, Memphis, and LA. I know a guy from Sioux City who's hitching in his wheelchair."

We must be running up a huge phone bill, but none of that seems to matter. "Don't worry," I remember telling Nick, "we'll pay them later."

We just keep calling and calling, telling everyone about our march, doing interviews, and writing press releases. We continue spreading the word and building momentum.

People seem to be calling from everywhere. Even my mother and father call from Massapequa, telling me that they will drive down in their motor home and hopefully be there for my birthday on the Fourth of July.

The folk singer Joan Baez helps raise money for us by holding a concert in Washington, DC. Several of us fly across the country to attend, and Joan makes sure we have seats right up front. She sings a number of very beautiful songs that night, and just as the concert is ending she tells the audience that she recently wrote a tune called "Where's My Apple Pie?" and is dedicating it to "the brave hunger strikers of the AVM."

As we sit in our wheelchairs listening to her sing, I look at the guys around me: Nick, Marty, Jafu, and Danny. We feel so special. There are tears in our eyes when she sings that song, and those haunting lyrics still resonate with me to this day. *"We've walked and wheeled from the battlefield, now where's our apple pie? . . ."* She tells everyone that night about the march, encouraging them all to get behind us. Joan becomes one of our biggest supporters and I remember promising her that night that we wouldn't let her down.

The concert reinvigorates us and we now throw ourselves even more into the march. Danny Prince's uncle Jerry contributes a few hundred dollars from his retirement fund, and eventually we are able to scrape up enough money to take several organizing trips, where Bobby, Joe Hayward, and I meet with veterans in Boston, New York, Chicago, and Washington, DC. We stay at their houses, sleep on their couches, and are constantly calling the press, trying to get the word out: TV, radio, newspapers—anyone who will listen to us. We return to LA more hopeful than ever.

The press loves it and are writing articles about us again and talking about what it might mean to have thousands of veterans descend on Washington. Several of the local TV stations show clips of the first Bonus March and even have a guy from the VFW saying that he's concerned about what we're about to do and that there could be trouble. Tony D., who for the most part was supportive of the march in the beginning, is now expressing his concern that things seem to be getting a bit out of hand and that we may be setting ourselves up for a fall—but regardless, we press on, and by early July of 1974 we are ready.

# Washington, DC

On the first of July, we all board a jet and fly to Washington, DC, landing at Dulles International Airport and checking in to a Holiday Inn not far from the White House. That night we discuss our plans. In three days we will all assemble about a mile and a half from the White House at Meridian Hill Park. The march will begin at two p.m., with the AVM leading the way in our wheelchairs, followed by members of the clergy, city officials, and veterans from all the wars. Our plan is to march straight down 16th Street to the White House, then set up our campsite in Lafayette Park.

I am still hoping for a great turnout. I remember feeling a bit anxious, unsure of how many would show up the next day. We have tried so hard. We've done everything we could, as far as I'm concerned, to make it a success. If the Bonus Army of 1932 was able to do it, then so can we!

As I lie on my makeshift bed in the hotel trying to fall asleep, I begin to visualize the march. I can see it all now: Nick, Woody, Willy, Bobby Mays, Danny,

Marty, and myself in the lead, carrying the AVM banner and American flag, wheeling down 16th Street,
tens of thousands of veterans stretching behind us for
miles.

I imagine the entire park filled with colorful tents
and flags where veterans from all of our country's wars
will come together. The wounded, the maimed, the
homeless, the destitute—they will all be there. It will
be flashed across every TV screen in America and soon
citizens from every walk of life will join us. Veterans
and their families will head to the nation's capital to
join the growing protest. They will fill the park, overflowing onto the streets, filling up Pennsylvania Avenue. Soon we will surround the White House. We will
become unstoppable—Willy, Danny, Bobby, Woody,
Marty, Nick, and myself. We will be in the lead, the
very tip of the spear, leaning forward in our wheelchairs, pressing our faces up against the White House
fence, passionate, determined, daring the government
and police to attack us, knowing full well what will
happen if they do, ready to sacrifice again, ready to risk
it all. The image of the police beating and dragging
away America's disabled veterans in their wheelchairs
in front of the White House on the Fourth of July will
infuriate everyone and soon the rebellion will spread
and become unstoppable, with the sound of helicop-
ter gunships overhead and bright flares lighting up the
night. The thousands of veterans behind us will push
forward, unafraid, outraged with the government and
its betrayal. I can see it all now: all of us together,

pushing up against that fence, demanding justice, demanding to be heard. "Let us in! Let us in! Let us in!" We will all grab hold of the fence, shaking it and shouting out in protest. Some will jump over, daring the security guards to stop them. Eventually the fence will collapse and waves of men will now step forward as if in battle, with the AVM leading the way toward the White House. Shots will ring out, but we will continue moving forward!

The following morning I still have no idea how many are going to show up but I continue to tell anyone from the press that we are expecting thousands—thirty thousand, fifty thousand, a hundred thousand!

Letting my imagination run wild, I go on and on, telling one reporter that the march will far exceed the one in 1932, making up one story and prediction after the next, always hinting at chaos, yet insisting it will be nonviolent. "This will be a peaceful march," I remember telling the reporter. Deep down inside I do not want violence, but I know that if it comes to that, the government will pay dearly.

I sense the reporter knows that the story I'm telling and the reality of what is now developing on the ground are two different things. He is sympathetic but I can detect in the tone of his voice a growing skepticism regarding the march. When I get off the phone I have a sinking feeling in the pit of my stomach that we've just about reached the end of the road. I think about what Tony D. said to me before we left

California, about how "every pipe dream has its day." That day, for myself and the AVM, may have finally arrived.

# The March

*July 4, 1974*

The day of the big march has finally come and it's clear from the very start that we are not going to get the numbers of veterans showing up that we hoped for. The air is hot and sticky, a typical summer day in the nation's capital. By eleven thirty, fewer than a hundred veterans and our supporters have arrived at Meridian Hill Park, and by noon our numbers have swollen to a measly one hundred and fifty.

Bobby and his little brother Charlie unfurl the thirty-foot AVM banner while Joe, Eddie, and Sharon hand out AVM membership cards and buttons to everyone. There are several American flags that were donated by one of the local VFW chapters and half a dozen red, white, and blue AVM flags on poles that we brought with us from LA. Some guy from Virginia in a Marine Corps dress blue uniform with a bugle keeps blowing "Taps" until we ask him to stop. A few local reporters show up and are milling about the crowd, doing interviews and asking questions as it becomes more and more clear that the Second American Bonus March is going to be a big bust.

I try to put on a brave face as one of the reporters walks up to me, asking where the tens of thousands of veterans I promised are. I don't know what to say other than realizing in this moment that the reality of the situation has finally caught up with me and there's no longer room for excuses. I can see by the looks of some of the others around me that they are becoming concerned. Joe Hayward is already joking about how the march is a farce and how this will be the end of the AVM.

I do my best to keep everyone's spirits up and some-time around two p.m. we begin to move down 16th Street. It's all getting a bit absurd as we shout and chant and try to look dignified. Marty and Nick are be-ing pushed by some of the other veterans and I do my best to maintain my composure. I don't know whether to laugh or cry and I feel ashamed and embarrassed as our sorry procession slowly rolls down 16th Street. I can't wait for the march to end.

The great crowds we hoped for are nowhere in sight. A few people on the sidewalk wave at us and I distinctly remember one old man getting up from his lawn chair and saluting. But for the most part people seem a bit puzzled by our ragtag procession as we head into Lafayette Park to set up our tents.

I am still hoping inside that the image of disabled Vietnam veterans camping out in front of the White House will inspire others to join us, but as we settle in, our dwindling numbers say it all. Fewer than fifty of the original marchers remain. Many say they are tired and want to go home, while others openly admit they are fed up because the march hasn't turned out the way they hoped it would.

Later that day, my mother and father drop by our campsite—just as they promised—having driven all the way from Massapequa and parked their motor home a few blocks from the White House.

"Happy birthday, Ronnie!" my mother shouts, giving me a great big hug and handing me a present. "You can open it later."

"We're really proud of you, Ronnie. Happy birthday," my father says softly, leaning over and placing his hand gently on my shoulder.

I am so happy to see them, and realize just how much I have missed them. They've always been there for me and have never let me down: praying for me at a special novena Mass at our church in Massapequa while I fought for my life on the intensive care ward in Da Nang; visiting me at the St. Albans Naval Hospital with other wounded marines; patiently caring for me when I was at the Bronx VA. They stood by me when I was arrested for protesting the war, and when I shouted down President Nixon with two other disabled veterans during his acceptance speech at the 1972 Republican National Convention in Miami. Even when our neighbors back in Massapequa rejected me, telling their children to stay away from me, afraid I might influence them with my "radical ideas"; and after the many nights I came home drunk from Arthur's Bar, tormented by the war, crying out and bitterly cursing God and my country, blaming God, blaming everyone.

My mother and father have never walked away, never abandoned me. They stood by me, continuing to love me despite my anger, suffering, and rage. They saw me through my sorrows, holding me in those dark moments when I felt so alone and wondered if anyone could ever understand, as I cried and shared with them the terrible things I had seen and done in the war. They had been and would always be there for me, and that gives me great comfort at a time when I feel so dejected about the failed march.

That evening I take them around our campsite, introducing them to all the guys, and even giving my mom an AVM button which she places proudly on her blouse. I try my best to act as if nothing's wrong, but a part of me wants to tell them how frustrated and embarrassed I feel. *What am I doing here with all these crazy people?* I think to myself. *I want to get out of here. I want to go with you and Dad back to Massapequa and leave all this madness behind,* I imagine saying to my mom. I need some peace and quiet away from all of this.

But I keep those thoughts to myself and feel sad as I watch my mother and father leave that evening, still wishing I could go with them. The Second American Bonus March has been an unmitigated disaster.

\* \* \*

Not long after my parents leave, I open the birthday present my mother gave me. It is a biography of President Franklin Delano Roosevelt, and my mother, in her perfect Catholic school cursive, has written an inscription inside: *Dearest Ronnie, I give you this book on your twenty-eighth birthday, July the Fourth 1974, with love in hopes that it will inspire you.*

I hold the book in my hands and can't help but think back to when my mother brought me another book, *Sunrise at Campobello,* a play by Dore Schary, while I was recovering at the St. Albans Naval Hospital in New York in 1968; it told of Franklin Roosevelt's great struggle with polio and ended with his inspiring speech at the Democratic Convention in 1924.

As night comes over our makeshift campsite, I transfer out of my wheelchair and onto my rubber mattress, and sometime around nine p.m. we all watch the great fireworks display above the Mall—rockets bursting in air, strings of firecrackers exploding, Roman candles popping, children with their sparklers turning night into day, reminding me of so many other Fourth of Julys when I was a boy growing up in Massapequa. Hundreds of thousands of people have traveled to Washington today to celebrate America's 198th birthday, but few if any know we are here.

After coming home from the war, the Fourth of July has always been a frightening day for me. It is no longer the celebration it once was. The terrible sounds and fury of the night's fireworks display now remind me of Vietnam—bullets cracking all around me, men being shot, men dying, my own wounding, the exploding sound next to my ear of the bullet that was to paralyze me for life. Independence Day has now become for me a night to simply endure, to take cover, to get into the house, shut all the windows and doors, turn up the TV really loud, place my fingers in my ears, and try to survive.

I snap back to the present as the explosions become less frequent, until finally it is quiet and another Fourth of July has ended.

As the days pass, fewer and fewer members of the media show up and we continue to lose hope. We are tired and dirty—none of us have showered. Tourists drop by and we explain to them why we are protesting, but my heart just isn't in it anymore. And I am not the only one. Arguments soon begin to break out as things become increasingly chaotic.

At one of our nightly meetings, a very frustrated Bobby Mays insists that we have to consider a change in tactics, and to my surprise, everyone agrees when he suggests we take over the Washington Monument. Tony D. quickly follows, proposing that we do a double takeover, or "two-pronged assault" as he is now calling it, where we will take over the Washington Monument and the White House at the same time. It will be a coordinated, nonviolent seizure of both national symbols by the AVM, with the demand to meet with the president to discuss the national veterans crisis. It is a bold move but what else is there to do? With the march now in a shambles we have to do something. And if we are ever going to reclaim our dignity and self-respect, this will be our last chance.

# We Take the Monument

The following morning, July 8, we fold up our tents, leave Lafayette Park, and take cabs over to the Washington Monument. I feel relief as we speed away. Within a few minutes we arrive and I look up at the monument which seems even taller and more impressive than ever. It is a beautiful day, and after purchasing tickets at a little kiosk, we get in line. I check my watch, knowing that Bobby and Tony D.'s group is now entering the White House tourist line.

I am feeling pretty good. Everything is going as planned and soon we are entering the monument and heading toward the elevator. None of the US Park Police seem suspicious of us. We are all trying to act like tourists, with Marty taking pictures with his little camera and Nick asking one of the rangers questions about the history of the monument. I instructed them all on the drive over to "blend in" and act like tourists, thus giving us cover and throwing off the park police. We get in the elevator and head straight to the top.

I check my watch again: eleven a.m.

When we finally reach the top and the elevator

door opens, I announce to everyone that we are Vietnam veterans and are taking over the monument to protest the poor treatment America's veterans are receiving in VA hospitals all over the country. Most of the tourists and the elevator operator seem surprised but immediately comply when Eddie politely escorts them to the stairwell for the long walk back to the ground level. I immediately hit a switch locking the elevator at the very top so it cannot be used.

As Joe and Eddie assemble all the wheelchairs in a semicircular defense position, I notice what appears to be an emergency phone inside the elevator and decide to see if I can get an outside line. To my surprise, after clicking the receiver a couple of times I am able to get an operator. "Hello, operator," I say, "I'm trying to reach the Associated Press. I don't have the number but if you would help me I'd really appreciate it." She is very nice and immediately connects me to the Associated Press office in Washington. "I've got an outside line!" I shout to the guys beyond the elevator. "She's connecting me right now to the Associated Press and I'm going to tell them everything that's going on here." I can't believe my luck. "Hello, Associated Press? This is Ron Kovic and we've just taken over the top of the Washington Monument! We're the same guys who took over Senator Cranston's office and went on the hunger strike . . . That's right . . . that's right!" I shout. "The Vietnam veterans who took over Senator Cranston's office. Seven paralyzed veterans, and our supporters have also taken over the White House. We demand to meet with President Nixon to discuss the national veterans crisis!"

The person on the other end of the line tells me he will send a reporter and photographer down to the monument. "By the way," he says, "did you know that those guys at the White House just took over the bathroom?"

I tell him I hadn't heard that and perhaps he's mistaken.

After that call, I click the receiver again to get an outside operator. I wonder how long I'll be able to keep using the monument's elevator phone before they shut it off. I keep calling the press, telling them about the takeover. I call CBS, NBC, the *Washington Post*, and even try calling the Washington Press Club where a guy says everybody is out to lunch and to call again later.

Each time I reach one of the news bureaus I shout to the guys outside the elevator, telling them who I have contacted. I decide not to mention what the guy from the AP told me about how he received a report that several AVM members have barricaded them-selves inside one of the White House bathrooms and are demanding to meet with President Nixon. It's em-barrassing. Of all the rooms they could have taken over in the White House, it had to be the bathroom. I re-member thinking to myself, *We're going to be a laughing stock. Why did they do that? Is there someone in the group who did this on purpose to embarrass us, to discredit us?*

By now Joe and Nick have hung the AVM banner

and American flag out one of the monument's small windows. After making all the calls I can, I join the others. I assume the elevator operator and tourists have made it to the bottom and are already alerting the authorities of our takeover.

We sit there for several more minutes until a park ranger who is terribly out of breath bursts through the door. I can still remember the look on his face. He is furious. As we all hold tightly to our chairs, he immediately turns the elevator back on, then shouts at us to get in. "You're all going to jail!"

But we refuse to move. "We're Vietnam veterans and we demand to speak with President Nixon!" I shout.

The ranger looks at me like I'm crazy and realizes that I'm probably the ringleader. He suddenly runs toward me, grabs the back handles of my wheelchair, and pushes me toward the elevator. I press down hard on my brakes, trying to keep the chair from moving, which seems to frustrate the ranger even more.

"I'm a paralyzed Vietnam veteran!" I shout.

As the chair rocks back and forth, he lifts it up from behind and dumps me onto the concrete floor. I can't believe it.

"I'm paralyzed, you motherfucker! Don't you realize I'm paralyzed?" I yell as I lie there sprawled out flat on my face.

Everyone seems to be screaming and cursing as a few more cops race through the door and surround us. Several other AVM brothers are beaten and tossed out of their wheelchairs. Danny Prince cries out that he can't move anything from his neck down. Joe Hayward sustains a sprained arm and bruise to his face when an enraged park policeman throws him to the floor.

When we finally get to the bottom of the monument, the press is already waiting—flashing their cameras as the park police wheel us away to the paddy wagons.

We spend the night in a DC jail and are released the following morning.

Bobby Mays and his team were a bit more fortunate. They spent a few hours locked in the White House bathroom, writing their demands on toilet paper, but got no response. When several tourists started complaining that they needed to use the bathroom, a compromise was reached and Bobby and his group were allowed to leave the White House at closing time without anyone being arrested.

We all meet up just as we planned at a coffee shop a block from Lafayette Park and have some breakfast, wondering what we will do next. After a few phone calls by Joe Hayward, we are told that we have a place to stay. About half an hour later we are driven to what Joe and Eddie are now referring to as a "safe house" in a rundown neighborhood a few miles south of the White House. It is here the AVM will set up its new base. The "owner" of the house, a former Black Panther and Vietnam veteran named Tyrone, says we can stay as long as we need to and that he and his "brothers" are supporting us all the way.

## The New York Times

July 9, 1974

### Veterans Demand to See Nixon; 4 Arrested at Capital Monument

WASHINGTON, July 9 (AP)—Protesters seeking a meeting with President Nixon to discuss veterans affairs locked themselves in a White House rest then in the West Wing conferring with his economic advisers.

The spokesman said that a member of the President's

---

The Weather

Today—Sun, high around 86, low in the 60s. Chance of rain 0 per cent today and tonight. Smarter—Rain, high in the 80s. Temperature range: Today, 61-85. Yesterday, 65-81. Details are on Page XX.

## The Washington Post

**FINAL**

168 Pages—6 Sections

Announcements D18  Garden  D-8
Classified       C25  Metro    B-1
Comics           D26  Obituaries D18
Crossword        D-6  Religion  D20
Editorials       A20  Sports    C-1
Food Diary       D10  Style    D-1
Financial        C-5  TV-Radio D-7

### Vote Is There To Impeach, Mansfield Says

By David S. Broder and Richard L. Lyons

Declaring that President Nixon's "dilatory tactics" have rebounded against him in Congress, Senate Majority Leader Mike Mansfield (D-Mont.) said yesterday that he now believes "the votes are there" in the House to impeach Mr. Nixon.

**RICHARD G. KLEINDIENST**

**Kleindienst Seen Plea Bargaining**

By Bob Woodward and Carl Bernstein

### U.S., Soviet Fail To Progress on Arms Limitation

**Hopes Dim For SALT Pact in June**

By Murrey Marder

LONDON, March 26 —

WHEELCHAIR PROTEST—Veteran Ron Kovic, left, and Max Wahlfall

Secretary of Defense Schlesinger talks to the press

---

The first thing I notice as we enter the house is the smell of mildew and piss. It is oppressively hot and there is no air-conditioning. There are several broken windows and from what Joe says, the house has been condemned. Revolutionary posters hang from its cracked and faded walls. A brightly colored Mao poster and a *Free Huey Newton* poster are neatly tacked up in the hallway, and the slogans *POWER TO THE PEOPLE* and *FUCK THE PIGS!* have been scrawled in what appears to be red lipstick just above the bathroom toilet. To say the least, the place is depressing, but we are in no position to complain. We are exhausted and welcome our new surroundings, simply grateful for a place to rest.

We all stay at the house for several days, but soon it becomes clear that our situation is quickly deteriorating.

"I wanna go home," says Marty.

"I've had enough of this shit!" says Nick.

Everything is a mess. I have come down with a low-grade fever from a bladder infection. Danny has already left with Sharon, quickly followed by Nick and Charlie. All sorts of new faces seem to be showing up at the house every day, people I have never seen before. I don't know who to trust. We try to maintain a sense of cohesiveness, still holding our nightly meetings, but it becomes apparent that things are once again falling apart.

# The Meeting

It all comes down to one last meeting on Thursday, July 11. Someone mentions they heard a rumor that there's going to be a "purge" of sorts. I immediately feel anxious as we form a large circle in the living room. Joe, Marty, Eddie, and Tony D. are still here, but there are new people as well, men and women who joined us at Lafayette Park and several others.

Bobby left for the coast yesterday, grumbling that the "Boner March," as he's now calling it, was a "big flop," and that he had to get back to LA in order to be with Danny and Sharon, who had left earlier in the week.

Joe Hayward is becoming more and more difficult to be around. He no longer calls me *brother* and is refusing to even make eye contact when we pass each other in the hallway. It seems as if he is someone else, a stranger, not the person I have known for so long. I am not sure what's going on. And while I know it probably sounds paranoid and crazy, I'm beginning to suspect that he might be scheming against me as I watch him spending lots of time with some of the newer, unfamiliar members of the AVM.

Those fears are bolstered when Jafu tells me he overheard Joe trashing me—telling some of the others that I'm on an "ego trip" and have to be dealt with. "I'd watch your back, brother," Jafu says. "I don't trust that motherfucker one bit. I've seen this shit come down before and it ain't pretty. He's either a cop, jealous, or hates your guts."

I thank Jafu for the information and tell him I'll be careful, but the truth is, his disclosure makes me even more nervous than before. I have long suspected Joe of being jealous of all the media attention I get, but I've never considered that he could be an undercover cop sent in to monitor me—someone sent to infiltrate and eventually dismantle the organization. At times throughout the hunger strike, I wondered about the possibility of someone among us being an informant for the police.

From my experiences over the years in the VVAW, I know the FBI and the cops regularly use informants to monitor, destabilize, and destroy politically active organizations. I, of course, never said anything to anyone at the time and barely even admitted it to myself, as I knew full well how that kind of suspicion and paranoia can quickly create distrust and break down the unity of a group. Wondering who the informant might be will always be in the back of your mind. And being betrayed like that by someone you trusted—thought was your friend—is something you never forget. So I try not to think about it too much, though I admit to myself that it's quite possible at this point that the AVM has been infiltrated.

I know that often the informant will become one of the most loyal and dedicated members—volunteering for everything, working harder than anyone else, trying not to act too smart or appear too inquisitive, playing along as best he can, while all the time collecting data—names, dates, behavior patterns. A truly effective informant will even move up over time in the organization into positions of leadership, carefully positioning him or herself, gathering intelligence, and fomenting dissent—turning members against each other. This tactic may have very well destroyed the Patients'/Workers' Rights Committee. I have been involved as an activist in the movement long enough to know that all of this is common practice. I had even once suspected my former girlfriend Carol of being an undercover agent.

After my first arrest in front of the Reelect Nixon headquarters in the spring of 1972, when I learned that two VVAW members were in fact undercover cops, I became even more aware of the government and FBI's dirty tricks. I had trusted the two undercover LAPD cops who infiltrated our demonstration that day in front of the Reelect Nixon office. Posing as long-haired VVAW members, they even offered to protect me and push my wheelchair. Their sudden and shocking betrayal later that afternoon, when they threw me out of my wheelchair, kicked me in the stomach, and tossed me, in handcuffs, into the back of a patrol car, was an experience I will never forget. At first I felt like a fool, before learning to carefully observe certain patterns of behavior, to trust my instincts, my intuition, and after

a while I got pretty good at spotting undercover agents
and cops.

And now, all those street smarts I picked up in my
days with the VVAW are once again at the forefront
of my mind. Could it be possible? Could Joe, who I've
trusted from the very beginning, be working for the
cops? Joe Hayward, who with his lovely wife Annie put
me up at their place on numerous occasions, going out
of their way to make me comfortable? *"Mi casa es tu
casa,"* Joe always said.

The meeting begins at exactly four p.m., with Joe announcing to everyone that we still have some "unfin-
ished business" to take care of. The look on his face is
grim and devoid of emotion. This only makes me feel
more anxious as my eyes dart from one unfamiliar face
to another. My mind races and I wonder who I can still
trust from our original group. All that unity and camaraderie I'd felt in Senator Cranston's office is slipping
away.

More than likely sensing trouble ahead, Tony D.
is the first to speak, encouraging everyone to respect
each other's points of view, saying that no matter what
"goes down," we are all brothers and the unity of the
AVM is the most important thing.

I try several times to catch Joe's gaze but he refuses
to look at me as he begins speaking in a strident tone.
"This is a meeting I have not been looking forward
to, but sometimes," he says, finally looking directly at
me, "when a brother gets out of line and attempts to

become a power unto himself, there is a need to discipline that brother, to contain him and, if necessary, silence him."

"Right on, brother!" a veteran shouts aggressively from a corner of the room, clenching his fists.

"You're fucking right, brother!" yells a long-haired homeless vet with a beer can in his hand who staggered into the house the day before.

"This afternoon we will be confronting a very serious problem in the AVM concerning one of our members who has strayed from the will of the group," continues Joe. "This is a matter of the utmost importance. As many of you know, these last few days—in fact, this last week to be exact—has been a bit disappointing for all of us. Many of you feel discouraged and frustrated that perhaps things didn't turn out the way you thought they would. A lot of promises were made and a lot of those promises were broken. I understand your frustration and, for many of you, your anger too. Certain individuals in our organization have let you down, and I think you would all agree that here in this room right now there is among us a brother who bears a great deal of that blame."

I watch as several heads in the circle bob up and down.

"There is no room in this organization for individualists or egomaniacs, no room for self-centered opportunists who only care about themselves," Joe says, raising his voice.

I quietly listen as he goes on, saying that I am "out

of control" and need to be muzzled, silenced like some rabid dog.

"The motherfucker lied to us!" shouts a voice from the corner. "He promised thousands were going to come!"

"He ain't no fucking leader!"

"He couldn't organize his way out of a paper bag!"

"He's nothing but a fucking fraud!"

"He let us down. Censure him, censure the motherfucker!"

"He's the reason for this failure and the brother needs to be punished. The fucker's guilty!" barks one guy.

"All he cares about is himself!" yells the guy's wife.

"Opportunist!" cries the homeless vet with the beer can, shaking his fist.

Tony D. suddenly stands up, shouting that Joe is completely out of line and has turned the meeting into a kangaroo court. "This isn't about reining in an individual! You've been jealous of this brother and scheming behind his back ever since you joined the AVM!"

"That's bullshit!" shouts Joe.

"Censure the motherfucker! The brother needs to be punished!" yells the homeless vet again.

Fights begin to break out as the meeting disintegrates into complete chaos. Still in a state of shock, my mind drifts as the accusations continue to fly—calling me a hustler, a liar who intentionally misled and deceived the members of the AVM.

"It's a fucking crucifixion!" yells Marty. "Don't you

guys realize what you're doing here? This brother's paralyzed and in a wheelchair. He started this whole thing. The AVM would be nothing if it hadn't been for him."

"Shut the fuck up," says a tall veteran standing by the kitchen door.

"You can yell all you want," Tony D. says calmly, "but you're not going to stop me from speaking." Suddenly the room becomes quiet—the rowdy group deciding to show some respect. "I don't know what's going on here today but I have a feeling . . . There are a lot of you in this room this afternoon who I have never seen before. A lot of you became members of the AVM in just the last few days. Some of you were with us on the Fourth of July when we marched on the White House, others joined us in Lafayette Park, while several of you joined us here at this house only yesterday. Don't you see what's happening here today?"

Before the blind marine can continue to appeal to their common sense, he is interrupted as the room breaks out into more chaos. Joe is clearly enjoying every minute of it and the room sounds more like a lynch mob than a group of rational men trying to work through their problems. And then, amid all the name-calling and accusations, I hear: "Call for a vote! Let's settle this fucking thing."

*Call for a vote?* I feel ripped apart.

"All in favor of removing Kovic from the AVM permanently and electing Joe Hayward as our new leader, raise your hands!" shouts Eddie.

Several hands shoot up across the room.

*Where are Bobby and Sharon when I need them?*

The only original members of the AVM who remain loyal to me that day are Marty, Willy, and Tony D., who refuse to raise their hands and will not vote me out of the organization.

"Calm down, everybody," Joe says with a smile, sensing the momentum shifting in his favor and enjoying the chaos he has created. He then calls for those who support me to raise their hands. As the hands go up, it becomes clear there's a tie. Then Joe explains in that sly voice of his that Nick, who'd left the day before, has assigned his proxy vote to him. Joe pulls out a signed note from Nick to prove this and then declares that according to Nick's wishes, he will cast one more vote, thus breaking the tie. Joe looks around sternly and announces, "As the newly elected leader of the AVM, I am now permanently dissolving the American Veterans Movement forever."

A brief cheer is quickly followed by silence as people start leaving the room. Tony D. tries to console me, gently placing his hand on my shoulder and mumbling in that philosophical way of his, "You can kill an organization, brother, but not an idea." I'm not really sure what he means but I thank him, grateful to have at least one true friend.

Saying that Vietnam veteran politics back then could be vicious is an understatement. A bunch of tormented Vietnam vets trying to act normal in a meeting often deteriorated into a shouting session, with some guys eventually freaking out. Many were suffering from

PTSD, and the group meetings could often turn into nightmarish sessions with bullying and belittling, with anyone in a leadership position ripped to shreds and humiliated.

Undercover cops might very well have been behind the meeting that day, but I will never know for sure how many of our so-called brothers were on our side or working for the police. Leaders in the veterans movement didn't last long. We trusted no one.

I feel punched in the stomach. The AVM is dead. The "collective" has spoken. *There is no room in this organization for individualists or egomaniacs* keeps playing over and over in my head. I barely said a word and now it's over. I sit there all alone, stunned and unable to move.

I have been banished from the AVM, an organization that I single-handedly created. I now fully understand what the expression *coup d'état* means.

Exhausted and feeling terribly betrayed, I catch a Greyhound bus up to New York the following day and stay with my friend Connie Panzarino. Connie does her best to comfort me as I lay my head in her lap and cry. I stay with her for several days until I finally decide to fly to Paris with what's left of my disability check. I hope to never return to the United States. Since the war, I have always dreamed of running away and becoming an expatriate, and now seems as good a time as any. I am angry, frustrated, and disgusted with everything that has happened.

It's a crazy trip lasting a little less than two weeks, with me flying to Paris and then traveling by train and ferry to England and Ireland. I meet wonderful people along the way, sometimes sharing stories of the AVM and the antiwar movement. It is exactly the escape I need to begin healing after all the drama with the collapse of the AVM. Soon, I feel strong enough to return home.

# Home

My friend and real estate agent Sally Baker picks me up at LAX airport and puts me up at her house in the canal section of Venice. She tells me her boss and my landlord, Eddie Menendez, is furious and looking for me. Apparently, I still owe him three months' rent and the telephone company has been calling him every day asking where his tenant is and who's going to pay the enormous bill. Sally tells me that Mr. Menendez sent people looking for me, scouring all the cafés along the beach, having heard a rumor I was back in town.

I hide out at Sally's place for a couple of weeks, resting up. Loyal to a fault, Sally promises not to disclose my location to her boss. "Last he heard, you were heading back to Ireland to live with the IRA," she tells me.

I decide one afternoon a few days later to call Tony D., he being one of the few people I feel I can still trust. He's happy to hear from me and begins updating me on all that happened while I was away. He explains how some of the guys kept living in my house on Hurricane Street after the AVM ended, and continued to use it as an organizing base. Tony says things got weird pretty quickly. Joe became really paranoid, telling everybody who chose to be a member of his newly formed group that they had to arm themselves for self-defense and become a more "vigilant" organization. Eddie volunteered to bring down his AR-15 rifle and a couple of shotguns, but that was voted down after a lot of arguing. Danny wisely pointed out that arming themselves would surely alienate their supporters and hurt the favorable relationships the AVM had developed with the press.

Eventually Mr. Menendez showed up, evicting everyone and taking away all the furniture, including my water bed, my old rolltop desk, and my typewriter—holding them hostage until I paid all the back rent that was due.

Before they left, one of the guys, whose name I'm not going to mention, apparently called everyone he knew, even making a call to an old girlfriend he met while on R&R in Taipei. Tony tells me they ripped the phones out of the walls when they took off and trashed the whole place until there was little left of the Hurricane Street house that had once been.

I ask Tony if my monthly compensation check ever arrived in the mail, and after pausing for a moment he tells me that Nick, more than likely with Joe's encouragement, forged my name on it and took it to the bank and cashed it, keeping all the money for himself. Ever since he got back from Washington, Tony tells me, Nick has been depressed and has started talking about suicide again. He has been in and out of the VA hospital psychiatric ward several times since the AVM fell apart.

I'm not too surprised when Tony tells me what Nick did. And as angry and violated as I have every right to feel upon hearing of his betrayal, I decide not to get upset. I tell Tony that even though I know what Nick did is wrong, I still love him and he will always be my brother. It's not as if I'm wanting or hurting—I have a place to stay and I know that my next check will be coming at the end of the month, for the rest of my life. I can depend on that check. I will always have my safety net, always have enough money to keep me above water. Nick, on the other hand, not being a service-connected veteran, doesn't have that kind of security. Paralyzed in a liquor store holdup in Compton, he will eventually spend all that money with no check coming in. Soon, all of it will be gone and Nick will be back out on the street sleeping in his station wagon in a parking lot in Venice by the pier. Nick did what he had to do to survive, and though I don't like it and know I will never be able to trust him again, I understand why he did it.

I make a sort of peace that day in my own mind, telling Tony that I have forgiven Nick and Joe for what they did to me, though I do fantasize driving my hand-controlled car down to Joe's place and doing something that I can't tell you about because if I did I'd get in a lot of trouble. Anyway, it doesn't really matter now because I never did it, and eventually the anger I felt toward him begins to fade the way it often does when we have terrible fantasies about people we want to get even with; those fantasies just end up petering out instead of becoming real. Thank God for that.

Marty started drinking again and Danny was talking about moving to Florida. Tony D. said that Willy Jefferson was back in the hospital on D ward. Bobby Mays had left Sharon and gotten in with a bad crowd, a bunch of blues musicians who were into heroin. He was still sarcastically calling our action the "Boner March," which really hurt my feelings. Tony told me he was on a downward spiral and had been arrested several times for drug possession.

I remember running into Bobby months later along the beach, barely recognizing him, gaunt face and sad-looking, so lost and gone. The heroin, cocaine, and speed had wasted his once-handsome young body and I remember feeling sad as I left him that day, a shell of the man he had once been. "Take care of yourself, Bobby," I told him before I pushed away in my wheelchair, not wanting to look back.

I pretty much stayed away from all of them during that period—keeping busy with my writing and trying my best to leave behind all the things that happened that spring and summer.

Eventually I left Sally Baker's house in Venice and found an apartment at the Santa Monica Bay Club on Pacific and 3rd Street, where I finally wrote that book I always promised myself I would write and even got it published to some pretty good reviews.

# Epilogue

I went back a few years ago, long after it had all ended and everyone had scattered and gone their separate ways, pushing my wheelchair down that quiet side street that ran along the ocean, back to Hurricane Street, where I sat in front of the old house for a long time, thinking of all the things that had happened there.

The place had changed a bit. There was a new paint job and a few shutters had been replaced, but it was still there—and I could see through all the layers of paint and time to the old house as it had once been when I first moved into the place back in the early spring of '74.

I'd hear word of the guys from time to time, rumors here and there, stories I overheard from some of the patients at the hospital whenever I went down for a visit, the usual scuttlebutt and gossip, but for the most part I still wondered what had become of all of them.

I was in New York City when I heard the news that Willy Jefferson had died of septic shock from a terrible bedsore that he could never seem to heal.

Jafu was next. He finally made it to Hawaii, where he got an apartment in downtown Honolulu not far from Waikiki Beach. He had only been there a few months when he died of a drug overdose. One of the guys at the hospital who knew him well told me he was buried at the Punchbowl National Cemetery with full military honors.

Danny Prince is still alive, last I heard, living somewhere in Florida.

Marty Stetson died a few years ago. They found his body in a rundown motel just outside the Long Beach VA. He was never able to heal his bedsore and from what I heard he was still drinking and had been hanging out with a dietitian named Mary Ellen, who was supplying him with drugs and alcohol. His friends stopped coming around after a while, complaining that his motel room stunk of feces and urine. In the end, he was all alone and even Mary Ellen left him, running away with his last disability check.

Nick Enders blew his brains out with a shotgun a few years ago. His brother called me, describing Nick's suicide in great detail. I didn't want to hear it and cupped the receiver, trying to block out the words. I did hear from one of the guys that Nick's Bronze Star, Purple Heart, and his dummy Edgar were placed in the coffin next to what was left of him, and were buried with him at the veterans cemetery in Westwood not far from the Federal Building.

After Sharon and Bobby Mays separated, Sharon moved to San Diego where she remarried and got a job as a nurse at a local hospital. I believe she still works there. She finally had that baby: his name is Tommy. He's thirty-nine now, has two kids, and lives somewhere in Texas, working at an auto parts store.

Bobby Mays eventually wound up in prison where he died of pneumonia. There was a ceremony held for him at Baker Beach in San Francisco, where his ashes were thrown into the ocean. It was not far from the Golden Gate Bridge, which he had threatened to jump off for years. Bobby's little brother Charlie got a job as a janitor at a local high school in Long Beach. He calls me from time to time, occasionally leaving rambling messages on my machine, mostly drunk and slurring his words, mumbling about how much he misses Bobby and the "old days with the AVM when we were all together." I keep telling him he's got to stop drinking or he'll end up like his brother, but he just doesn't seem to want to listen.

Tony D. became a philosophy professor at USC and still calls me from time to time. He got married to a beautiful woman named Marie about a year ago and now lives in Long Beach.

I got a call from Joe Hayward a few years ago telling me that he and Annie had broken up and that he was living alone on the USMC base at Camp Pendleton, renting a small trailer by the ocean. He told me he liked being around other marines. "It feels like home," he said with a sad laugh. I remember having a feeling right after we got off the phone that we would never talk again, and we never did.

\* \* \*

I still go down to the hospital from time to time. There are a lot of new faces there now. A whole new generation of severely maimed are returning from Iraq and Afghanistan, young men and women who were not even born when I came home wounded to the Bronx VA in 1968.

The horrors and nightmares of war have followed them home, just as they did my generation. Many suffer from PTSD. Thousands are homeless. In a 2013 article, the *Washington Post* cited a VA study that found an average of twenty-two veterans commit suicide *per day*. Of this staggering number, roughly a third are under fifty, suggesting they are our young Iraq and Afghanistan war veterans. Tragically, VA hospitals around the country often continue to fail to provide the timely care these veterans need, turning them away or forcing them to wait for weeks at a time for help.

I sometimes see these young veterans in the hallway sitting in their wheelchairs seeming lost, reminding me of how it had been for us years before. I feel close to them. Though many years separate us, we are brothers and sisters. They are at the very beginning of dealing with their paralysis just as we were back in 1968. It is all new to them and they have much to learn, just as we once did. It will be a long and difficult road for them and I can't help but wonder how many will make it through the years to come.

They tore down the old SCI building several years ago and replaced it with a center for blind veterans, building a beautiful new Spinal Cord Injury complex next door.

Most of the aides and nurses from the old wards have gone and have been replaced by all sorts of new faces.

Dr. M. retired years ago. He's well into his eighties now, and I hear he's become a bit frail and his eyesight is failing. One of the aides told me that he occasionally still walks the SCI wards late at night with the help of his granddaughter, checking up on his boys.

I have a new doctor now; he's Vietnamese American. He saved my life last spring. He told me that I came pretty close to dying of pneumonia. I was on the intensive care ward for nearly a week. It took me several months to recover but I'm doing a lot better now. I do deep-breathing exercises every night to keep my lungs strong.

Most of the guys who opposed me during those years aren't around anymore, having either died or moved on. For a long time after the strike ended, I felt anxious every time I went down to the hospital, thinking someone was going to start yelling at me, cursing me out, or threatening my life, but I don't worry about that too much anymore. Four decades is a long time.

A few years ago, I was contacted by a reporter from the *Los Angeles Times* telling me that Donald Johnson had died of complications from cancer in Fredericksburg, Virginia, asking me for a quote for his obituary that was due to be published the next day. Carefully choosing my words, I told the reporter that after the strike had ended, "Johnson began to develop a new understanding and awareness" of the needs of Vietnam veterans and he had pushed hard for improvements in VA facilities.

After we got off the phone, I thought about how I hadn't been completely honest with the reporter and had withheld a lot of my true feelings about Mr. Johnson that I was still afraid to share.

I couldn't help but think back to the last time I had seen him, several years after the strike ended, when I was lobbying for veterans' rights in Washington, DC. I remember spotting him late one afternoon as I was crossing the street on my way to the Capitol, standing all alone on the corner seeming so sad and lost. I slowly approached him. "Mr. Johnson," I said, "I don't know if you remember me, but my name is Ron Kovic and I was one of the Vietnam veteran hunger strikers in Senator Cranston's office who met with you back in 1974." He seemed surprised as I reached out to shake his hand. "I just want to thank you, Mr. Johnson, for everything you've done for our veterans."

Neither one of us said much after that and we soon parted ways. I watched him slowly walk away, crossing the street the way ordinary people do, and disappearing. It was the first time I think I allowed myself to see him as a real person, and not the cardboard image we had created during the strike. In the intervening years, I would discover that he had served honorably during World War II as a sergeant in General George Patton's

3rd Army in Europe, receiving both a Bronze Star and Purple Heart. He had told me his father had died in World War I, and his foster father was disabled in that war. His son was a disabled Vietnam-era veteran.

Never during the strike did I or the others take this into consideration. How could we? We were angry . . . obsessed with our own priorities. Back then there was no middle ground. The truth is, I wish I had been able to tell him that day that I was sorry for the way we had treated him. No longer was he the hated enemy, the despised bureaucrat we had relentlessly attacked and vilified for over two weeks in Senator Cranston's office.

I felt a bit sad thinking of Johnson and all the others who had died, of my own mortality and how soon all of us who were involved in the great drama that unfolded that spring would be gone, with nothing left but a few faded memories and entries I had made in my diary.

# Postscript

*January 20, 2015, Bed 18*

I'm back in the VA hospital again. I really had no other choice. My arms and shoulders finally gave out after decades of overuse. Years of lifting myself in and out of my wheelchair have taken their toll. I lost my grip falling out of bed a few weeks ago and lay on the floor for nearly an hour before help finally arrived.

The doctors tell me that surgery isn't an option and there's not much more they can do other than occasional Cortisone shots in my shoulder, which don't seem to make much of a difference. They tell me that what's happening to me with my shoulders is quite common with those of us fortunate enough to have survived all these years in a wheelchair.

I will need to hire a caregiver and the VA will provide a battery-operated lift and sling to assist me in and out of my bed when I get home. It's okay for me to finally admit I need a little help. I'm very proud that I've lasted as long as I have and that I've been independent for so many years. I know how lucky I am to still be alive while so many others that I once knew are now gone.

This will be a bit of an adjustment after years of living independently and not having to rely on anyone for help. For now, I will have to count on the aides here on the paraplegic ward to assist me and I'm grateful for that. They're taking good care of me, getting me in and out of bed each day, bathing me every morning, helping me get dressed, even buttoning my shirt. I've been losing the feeling in my hands and fingers for some time now. I was diagnosed with carpal tunnel syndrome a few years ago but only recently have I had to ask others for help. Though many problems still exist throughout the VA hospital system, at least here on SCI ward T-2 things seem to have changed. I definitely notice the difference. The aides are much more polite and professional and I hear a lot of the troublemakers from the past have either retired or been let go. People now seem to genuinely care.

Several of the new caregivers who have begun working here recently are young veterans from the wars in Iraq and Afghanistan who tell me they are grateful to be serving their fellow veterans. They do my bowel care every few days and change my catheter every two weeks. For years I changed my own catheter and did my own bowel care, but as time has passed it has become more and more difficult, due to the growing weakness in my hands and shoulder pain. I don't feel sorry for myself and have few regrets and no longer grieve like I did back in '68 when I was so young and my wounding was still new to me.

The only thing that is important to me now is getting out of this hospital room each day and having some semblance of normalcy in my life. A man needs his dignity no matter how much he has lost. I am so grateful to be alive.

I spend most of my mornings racing through the hallways in my electric wheelchair. Veterans pass me as I move along. Almost every afternoon I find myself at the recently completed Patriot Café where I have lunch and sit with other wounded veterans from all our country's wars.

Today, bright sunshine streams in from large plate-glass windows, filling the room with light and healing. It is a beautiful and spacious setting and obviously someone has put a lot of time and care into designing the new place.

An elderly World War II veteran who can no longer use his hands is fed by his wife. A Korean War veteran missing a leg reads his newspaper, while a young Iraq War veteran in a bright blue hospital gown limps past me with his mother. Vietnam veterans sit together at their favorite table in the back of the café, seeming old before their time. It is a comforting feeling to be with all of them.

After lunch I go to a small patio in the back of the café. It is a quiet, park-like setting where patients and other hospital personnel sit under umbrellas at small tables eating their lunch and enjoying the day. Bright yellow chrysanthemums line the walkway. The scent of pine and eucalyptus trees fills the air. I close my eyes and take a deep breath, feeling the warm sun on my face, and for a moment I almost forget I'm in a hospital.

Several years ago, the Long Beach Military Order of the Purple Heart donated a small granite memorial that was placed in the center of the patio of the Patriot Café to honor America's military personnel killed or wounded in combat. It is a very beautiful memorial depicting the Purple Heart and I often find myself sitting before it reflecting on the words etched into its surface:

*Dedicated to those who gave their blood for our country knowing that wounds suffered in combat by American servicemen and women is a cost of freedom. This medal is distinguished by those who gave some and some who gave all for peace in our time.*

As I carefully reflect on these words, I close my eyes and can now clearly see all their faces once again as if it was yesterday: Woody, Marty, Bobby Mays, and all the rest who came to fight a great battle against an enemy not thousands of miles from home but here within our own land.

Later in the day I return to my room where I sit alone waiting for my caregiver to help lift me back into bed.

As the evening comes on and the room grows darker, my thoughts once again return to that spring long ago when we were young and the war was still within us, and how for one brief moment we all came together and won a great victory.


## The End

# Acknowledgments

First, I'd like to thank my publisher Johnny Temple, who believed in the book from the very beginning. His enthusiasm, support, and exceptional skills as an editor helped to make the book what it is today.

Thanks also to Johanna Ingalls, who despite her busy schedule always took the time to listen. Her suggestions and editorial assistance proved to be invaluable toward the completion of the book.

I'd also like to thank Ibrahim Ahmad and Aaron Petrovich for their advice, especially Ibrahim's suggestion that I add a few paragraphs "set firmly in the present day" and discuss ongoing problems with returning veterans and their care—problems which still exist to this day with VA hospitals.

And lastly, I want to thank my dear sweet love, TerriAnn Ferren, who on that beautiful morning long ago listened as I told her the story of *Hurricane Street*, of Willy and Bobby and all the others; and who immediately insisted that I had to write the book. You, my love, have been a constant source of inspiration, love, and support. Clearly the book could have never been written without you.